Mosdos Press
Cleveland, Ohio

Silver

A COLLECTION OF SHORT STORIES

MOSDOS PRESS
Literature Series

Editor-In-Chief
Judith Factor

Graphic Design
Gila Morgenstern

Curriculum
Jill Brotman

Text Editor
Abigail Rozen

Copy Editor
Laya Dewick

Design Advisor
Carla Martin

Text and Curriculum Advisor
Rabbi Ahron Dovid Goldberg

Table of Contents

Act of a Hero   Hugh Garner 5

Mick Harte Was Here   Barbara Park 13

Come of Age   B. J. Chute 23

Of Missing Persons   Jack Finney 41

The Gold Medal   Nan Gilbert 55

The Long Winter   Walter Havighurst 65

Lost Sister   Dorothy M. Johnson 81

Father and the "1812"   Todd Rolf Zeiss 97

The House Guest   Paul Darcy Boles 113

The Bet   Anton Chekhov 123

Going to Run All Night   Harry Sylvester 133

Stop the Sun   Gary Paulsen 149

Consider This...

At the core of nearly every story is a conflict.

What is a conflict? A conflict is a clash. A conflict shows the coming together of opposing forces or wills or ideas—of two or more things that do not mix—like the old expression about oil and water.

Particularly in fiction, we read about characters who have a struggle and whose struggles must be resolved by the end of the tale. The conflict is what catches our interest. In fact, in storytelling, the suspense comes from waiting to see if the conflict will be resolved. Moreover, we wait to see if it will be resolved *to our satisfaction*!

Act of a Hero is about a man who struggles with himself. When he does not do what one part of him thinks he should do, he feels he is a coward. In truth, by story's end, the conflict is not resolved. It surely is not resolved, as we would hope it to be.

Hugh Garner

Act of a Hero

George Ellsworth drove slowly along the small town's main street, waving occasionally to people he knew on the sidewalks.

The winter morning was cold and brisk, and the tires of his stakebody truck crunched on the snow. Now and then he hunched his long frame above the wheel as he shifted his position on the seat. Above his smooth thirty-year-old face his ski-cap was pushed back to release a few locks of taffy-colored hair, which hung on his forehead like a boy's.

While his truck was being loaded with flour at the mill, he had stepped across the street for a coffee, and now he felt warm and at peace with the world. If nothing delayed him, he could drop off his load at the freight sheds and be back home in time for an early lunch.

He left the business blocks of Main Street behind him and rolled down the hill to the residential section[1] of town. As he approached the public school, he glanced in its direction; several small children spilled from the front door of the school into the street. He slowed his truck, hoping to catch a glimpse of his own youngsters, Barry and Sandra, when they emerged too for what he thought must be morning recess.

When he drew abreast of the school, a larger group of youngsters shot from the doorway and tumbled down the front steps into the snow. They picked themselves up and ran around in frenzied[2] circles, shouting and pointing to the doorway, from which a steady stream of pupils and

1. *residential* (REZ ih DEN shul) *section*: the area of a city in which there are houses, not businesses
2. *frenzied* (FREN zeed): full of panic and urgency

teachers were hurrying. Now he noticed, for the first time, that none of them were wearing their outer clothing, despite the cold. The reason became apparent immediately as a heavy red-tipped cloud of smoke burst from a window at the side of the building. He twisted the wheel and pulled the truck into the curb.

As he ran across the sidewalk, he met Mr. Manning, the principal. "Children trapped!" Manning pointed without halting his headlong rush. "Got to phone—firemen—across the street!"

George felt his body slump as if it was suddenly drained of blood. He shoved his way through the screaming crowd of children, trying to spot the faces of his own son and daughter. As he stumbled about, unable to see them, his fear grew to panic, and he began shouting their names above the hubbub about him.

Now and then, youngsters, singly or in hand-holding pairs, groped their way through the doorway, wiping their eyes and screaming with fright, before rushing down the front steps into the crowd. These children were much younger than the ones he had first seen running from the building, and George remembered with horror that the kindergarten classroom was situated at the rear of the old building. It was the room in which his youngest child, Barry, was a pupil.

Clawing his way through the mob of children he reached the front steps. The front door opened and out of a choking cloud of heavy smoke came the kindergarten teacher, carrying a little girl in her arms. Clinging to her skirts and to each other were four other youngsters, their faces gray and their eyes wide-staring despite the acrid smoke. None of them were his own two children.

He grabbed the young kindergarten teacher by the arm. "Are there any more inside!" he screamed at her.

She nodded, coughing. "I lost some, I'm afraid."

He pulled open the heavy door and ran headlong into the smoke-filled hallway. Ahead of him, showing beneath the billowing clouds of smoke, were two small girls, running across the hallway or corridor from one classroom to another. Farther along, towards the rear of the building, one wall was blazing. There was a sound like the whimpering of wounded dogs.

He peered[3] into the two empty classrooms nearest him, then bent low as he ran along the corridor to another classroom, into which he had seen the two little girls disappear a moment before. This room was almost free of smoke, and the two children were climbing to the top of the radiator so they could reach the catch on a window. They were in no immediate danger from either the flames or smoke, and George knew they would be rescued as soon as they were seen from outside.

He turned from the classroom door and saw that the flames had now scaled the wall and were licking their way across the ceiling. On their trailing edge, large sheets of wallboard were hanging like fiery stalactites,[4] curling and undulating[5] in the intense heat. When he drew closer to the fire the heat engulfed him in a nauseating wave, and turning his head away, he groped for the parka on his sheepskin jacket and pulled it over his head.

In order to reach the rear of the corridor, where he felt certain his own children were trapped, he would have to run the gauntlet[6] of the flames. It flashed through his mind that he had often thought of rescuing a family from a burning house, especially if it was his own. It had seemed such a simple fundamental act of manhood when he had thought of it. Now, facing the painful, stabbing flames that barred his path, and choking on the heavy smoke, he hesitated. From behind the fire came the sobbing cries of the trapped children, their screams muted[7] now by the crackling roar of the nearby flames.

He edged slowly into the burning section of the corridor, but a quick stabbing flame reaching towards his face made him retreat. *I'm a coward*! he realized suddenly through the panic that now closed in on him. *Now, the one time in my life when I need courage, I have none!*

---

3. *peered*: looked into searchingly

4. *stalactites* (stuh LAK tyts): a deposit of calcium carbonate shaped like an icicle often found hanging from the roofs of caves

5. *undulating* (UN dyuh lay ting): moving with a wavelike motion

6. *run the gauntlet* (GAWNT let): a form of physical punishment in which an offender was made to run between two rows of men who beat him with sticks or weapons as he passed; the expression is used to describe someone who must pass through a very dangerous situation

7. *muted* (MYOOT ed): muffled; quieted

With a coward's clarity he rationalized, *Perhaps my kids have already reached the yard*, excusing his fear and hesitation. There was only the slightest chance of getting through to the children on the other side of the fire, and if he failed it would mean the loss of *his own* life as well as theirs. And it was quite probable that they would be rescued by the firemen through the rear windows of the school.

That morning at breakfast young Barry had asked, "Can I go out in the truck with you this afternoon, Daddy?" G-d! He took a step towards the fire once again, fighting the cowardly voice of reason that told him to turn and run.

Can I go out with you this afternoon, Daddy? Of course! Of course! Now he remembered. The children had stayed home from school today so their mother could take them to the dentist. They weren't in the blazing school at all, but back in the center of town at the dentist's office! Oh, dear G-d! Suddenly the conflicting[8] fears and hesitations dropped their weight from his heart.

When he once again noticed the fire, his estimation of his chances of getting through it had become impersonal, and now the space between the burning piles of wallboard and wood paneling had narrowed considerably. It would be almost impossible to crawl or run between them without being burned. The sobbing of the trapped children and the noise of the fire were suddenly dimmed in his ears by the rising wail of sirens from the street, showing him that the fire trucks had arrived. He was no longer forced to make a decision, and he backed away from the flames and smoke with hurried stumbling eagerness.

As he hurried back along the corridor, he glanced into the room where he had last seen the two little girls. They were standing on a ledge, silhouetted[9] against the window, and had almost succeeded in opening a space large enough to crawl through.

He had to accomplish something to justify his frightened return to the outside. He ran between the desks and picked both children from the window ledge, and with one beneath each arm hurried out of the room and along the corridor to the front door.

---

8. *conflicting* (kun FLIK ting): differing; being in disagreement
9. *silhouetted* (SIL oo ETT ed): outlined; only their shape shown

As he emerged from inside the building, there was a loud cheer from the children on the lawn and from the thickening crowd of adults who were approaching the school along the street. Several cars parked along the curbs gave him an accolade with their horns.

He set the two little girls on their feet in the snow, and allowed the teachers and some newly arrived parents to pump his arm and shout their thanks in his ear. When he remembered the children still trapped at the rear of the building, he shouted the information to a passing fireman.

Much later, after being interviewed briefly by a young man from *The Clarion*, the local paper, he was able to drag himself away from the admiring crowd that now surrounded him. The fire was out, and the trapped children in the kindergarten class had all been rescued by the firemen. The schoolchildren had been formed into classes, and the only casualty was a small boy who had been overcome by smoke.

As George climbed into his truck he heard the principal shout, "Now, children, let's give three cheers and a tiger for Mr. Ellsworth!" With the children's cheers echoing like a mockery behind him, he stepped on the gas and pushed the truck as fast as he could away from the school.

He took his time unloading the flour at his destination, and drove as slowly as he could on the way home. When he arrived at his house in the late afternoon, the kitchen table was set, and his smiling wife and children came to the back door to meet him.

After making himself ready for supper, he sat down at the table and glanced up into the beaming face of his wife. She pointed in front of him at the open newspaper propped against the sugar bowl. There was a photograph of himself coming down the school steps with the two little girls under his arms, and a headline over the story of the fire that read, THE ACT OF A HERO. He swept the paper from the table to the floor.

"Are you mad, Daddy?" Sandra asked, in open-mouthed wonder.

He stared down at his plate, unable to face his wife and children.

"Why are you mad, Daddy?" his daughter asked again.

It was an unanswerable question. It was a question he would be unable to answer for the rest of his life.

Thinking It Over

1. What does the kindergarten teacher say, when George Ellsworth questions her? Does her response have the tone you would expect?

2. Mr. Ellsworth sees "two small girls" enter a classroom. Why doesn't he help them? Do you think his reasoning is sound?

3. What had George often thought about previously? Why did he have such a fantasy?

4. George reasons that perhaps his children have already gotten out. Would that excuse his leaving without trying to help the other children?

5. Why is George mad at the end of the story? Should he be?

Consider This...

The character named in the title of this story, Mick Harte, never actually appears. The story is narrated by his sister. She tells a story in which she circles around the heart of the conflict—his death.

If you have ever been a part of a tragic event, one that can never be changed, you will not be surprised by what is at the core of her grief. When we lose someone, we often fill the empty space that person leaves with self-torment: what we could have done or what we should have done for the one whose absence is almost too hard to bear.

Barbara Park

Mick Harte Was Here

Mick Harte was a good-natured, funny boy who liked to joke with his family. But when a bicycle accident ends his life, his family is devastated. Each of them must deal with their loss in their own way. His sister, Phoebe, is angry—angry with Mick, the people around her, and herself.

Three blocks from my house, there used to be a dangerous intersection. It was one of those intersections where it was impossible for cars to pull out onto the main street without horns honking and brakes screeching and stuff.

My father griped[1] about it every time we drove through there.

"The city's not going to put a light in here until someone gets hurt," he'd say. "You wait and see. It's going to take an accident before anything gets done."

Last year there were four accidents in seven months and they finally installed a traffic signal.

The first time we drove through it, some guy ran a red light and Pop had to swerve out of the way to keep from hitting him.

It scared us both to death. Pop swore at the guy and then started right in on this lecture about "how you can lead a horse to water, but you can't make him drink."[2]

---

1. *griped*: [slang for] complained
2. *you can lead a horse to water but you can't make him drink*: an expression meaning: you can give a person the opportunity to do something, but you can't make him do it

"It's a sad lesson, Phoebe," he said. "But no matter how many traffic lights they put in, they'll never be able to make people use common sense and good judgment."

As he was talking, he turned around to make sure I was paying attention. While his head was turned, our car drifted into the next lane and two cars blasted their horns at us.

He made a quick recovery. It was close, though.

It was also the end of his talk on good judgment and common sense. And the lesson I ended up learning that day was that even smart guys with chemistry degrees do stupid stuff once in a while.

It's just that usually when you do stupid stuff, you luck out and get away with it. And if you luck out enough times, it's pretty easy to start believing that you're always going to luck out. *Forever*, I mean.

Like I can't even count how many soccer games I played in without shin guards before I finally got kicked in the leg and started wearing them. Over thirty, though, I bet.

And my mother had never had a major sunburn her whole entire life till she and Pop went to the beach for their anniversary last year. You can still see the blotchy places where her skin peeled from all the blisters, by the way.

And then there was Mick. Who went twelve years and five months without ever falling off his bike.

So he refused to wear a helmet.

And it's the one thing about him that I've tried to forget. And to forgive him for.

And I'm sorry, but I can't seem to do either one.

It was over a week before Mrs. Berryhill called me down to her office again. I was kind of nervous when I got her note. Even though I knew my parents had explained to her about me ditching school that day, part of me was still expecting detention.

That's why I was relieved to see another woman sitting in her office when I walked in. Mrs. Berryhill introduced us. Her name was Mrs. Somebody-or-other from the PTA.

She shook my hand and said how "sincerely sorry" she was about what happened to my brother. Then she started right in on how the PTA wanted to make sure that nothing like that ever happened again, so they were going to sponsor this big assembly on bike safety. It was already in the works, she said. There were going to be police officers, and instructional videos, and demonstrations of the latest safety gear, and yadda, yadda, yadda...

"We'd like to invite you to sit onstage with the other speakers," she told me. Then she shook my hand again and asked if I thought maybe I could say a few words to my classmates about bike safety. Because a few words from me would have "a tremendous impact," she thought.

And through all this, I just sort of sat there, you know? Staring at her in disbelief. Because I swear I could not figure out what planet this woman had come from.

I mean where in the world had she ever gotten the nerve to ask me something like that? Had it never even dawned on her that the timing of a bicycle-safety assembly was just a little off for me? That maybe I would have liked to see a safety assembly *before* my brother was killed?

I didn't make a scene. I just stood up and took my hand away.

"I can't," I said.

When I turned to go, Mrs. Somebody-or-other fell all over herself telling me how much she understood.

Which really killed me, by the way.

Because the woman didn't have a clue.

I don't know when I changed my mind about speaking at the assembly.

I think it was just one of those flipflops you do sometimes. You know, like at first you have this gut reaction to something and you're positive that you're totally right. Only after a while, it creeps into your mind that the other guy may actually have a point. Then the next thing you know, his point's making more sense than your point. Which is totally annoying. But still, it happens.

It used to happen with me and Mick all the time. Like a couple of months ago, we were arguing about whether the Three Stooges were funny or not. I kept saying they were hilarious, and Mick kept saying they were just morons.

Then we started kind of wrestling around a little bit, and the next thing I know, Mick jumps up and starts slapping the top of his head with his hand and fluttering it up and down in front of my face. After that, he grabs my nose with his fist, twists it hard, and finally slaps it away with his other hand. He ended his performance with the classic Three Stooges laugh—Nyuk, nyuk, nyuk—and a quick move to boink my eyes out with his fingers. Fortunately, I was able to block it with my hand.

Mick stopped the routine as fast as he had started it. Then, without saying a word, he stood up real dignified-like and dusted himself off.

He looked at me without the trace of a smile. "Hilarious, wasn't I?" he said dryly.

"Yes," I lied. "You were."

But deep down I had already started to feel different about the Stooges.

There were eight hundred people in the gym when I walked to the microphone that morning. I wasn't nervous, though, which really surprised me. But I swear I felt almost relaxed when I set down my bag of stuff next to the podium.

"I'm Mick Harte's sister," I said. Then I bent down and reached into my plastic bag.

"When Mick was in third grade, this is what my grandmother from Florida sent him for the holidays."

I held it up. "It's a glow-in-the-dark bow tie with pink flamingoes on it." A couple of kids chuckled a little.

"Don't worry," I said. "He never wore it. He said it made him look like a dork."

There was more laughing then. And I reached into my bag again.

"When Mick was in fourth grade, my Aunt Marge sent him this from Michigan."

I held up a hat in the shape of a trout.

"Mick said this one went beyond dork, all the way to doofus," I said.

This time everybody really cracked up. Some of the kids in the first row even stood up and started craning their necks to see what I would pull out next.

They watched as I turned the bag upside down and a cardboard box fell onto the stage.

Carefully, I set it on the podium and waited for everything to get totally quiet.

"When Mick turned ten, my parents gave him this for his birthday."

I took my time opening the lid. I mean you could really feel the anticipation and all.

But when I finally pulled Mick's gift out of the box—still brand-new—there was just this gasp.

And no one laughed at all.

No one even moved.

"This was my brother's bike helmet," I said.

My voice broke, but somehow I forced myself to finish.

"He said it made him look like a dork."

I don't know if what I said at that assembly will make a difference. I don't know if it will help anyone use better judgment than my brother did. I hope so, though…Because Mick died from a massive head injury. And yet the doctors said that just an inch of Styrofoam would have made the difference between his living and dying.

It's been a month since the accident now. Things have gotten a little better at home. Nana from Florida went back to Orlando. And my mother gets dressed in the mornings, usually. She's gone back to work, too—just two days a week, but it's a start.

We sit down to dinner every night at our new places. Eating still isn't a big deal with us, though. Like last night we had grilled cheese sandwiches and mashed potatoes. And on Sunday all the forks were in the dishwasher so we ate potato salad with soup spoons. My mother's eased up on stuff like that. Death sort of gives you a new outlook on the importance of proper silverware.

It's called *perspective*. It means your father doesn't iron a crease in his pants every morning. And the hamburgers come in all shapes and sizes.

I've started to laugh more often. But I still feel guilty when I'm having too good a time. Which is totally ridiculous. Because if I want to feel guilty, there're lots better reasons than that. Like I'm just now starting to deal with how Mick asked me to ride his bike home that day and all.

I kept that whole memory tucked away in the back of my mind after the accident happened. But bad memories must grow in the dark, I think, because it kept on creeping in my thoughts, till it was with me almost all the time, it seemed.

Then last Saturday, when my father and I were riding home from a soccer game, my stomach started churning like it always does right before I'm about to blurt out an unplanned confession.

It's one of the sickest feelings there is, by the way. To realize you're about to squeal on yourself like that.

The only thing sicker is keeping it inside.

So it all came busting out. All about how Mick asked me to ride his bike that day. And how I had soccer practice so I told him I couldn't do it.

"See, Pop? Don't you get it? I could have kept the accident from ever happening. If only I had ridden his bike home, Mick would still be here right now."

I was crying a little bit now. But except for handing me the travel tissues from the dashboard, my father hardly seemed to notice. Instead, he just kept staring out the window at the road in front of us.

Then slowly, he began shaking his head from side to side.

"I'm sorry, Pop. I'm sorry. I'm sorry," I said over and over again.

My face was buried in my hands when I finally felt him touch my shoulder.

"I'm going to make a list, Phoebe," he said. "And I want you to keep a count." His voice was real low and steady as he began.

"*If only* you had ridden Mick's bike home, Mick would still be here.

"*If only* the truck had been going a little faster or a little slower, Mick would still be here.

"*If only* his meeting had been scheduled one day earlier or one day later, Mick would still be here.

"*If only* it had been raining that day, I'd have driven him to school and Mick would still be here.

"*If only* one of his friends had kept him talking a second longer at his locker that afternoon...

"*If only* the house he was riding to had been in the other direction...

"*If only* that rock hadn't been on the sidewalk at the exact spot..."

He stopped then. And I was pretty sure he was finished. But all at once, he heaved this... awful sigh and whispered, "If only I had made him wear his helmet."

My heart broke for my father at that moment, and I reached my hand out to him.

He held on to it tight. Then he smiled the saddest smile you've ever seen.

"What number are we on, little girl?" He sounded so old.

I scooted closer to him.

"I think we're done, Pop," I said softly.

He pressed my hand to his cheek.

The two of us drove home in silence.

Thinking It Over

1. Compare the father's attitude at the beginning of the story (for example, when he says, "...they'll never be able to make people use common sense and good judgment") with the position in which he finds himself at the end of the story. What can we learn from this?

2. Why is Phoebe asked to participate in the bike safety assembly?

3. Can the PTA make sure that an accident like Mick's never happens again?

4. What does Phoebe mean when she says that the woman from the PTA doesn't have a clue?

5. Why is the climax of the story the father's whispering, "'If only I had made him wear his helmet'"?

Consider This...

The expression, *come of age*, is an expression that means, "mature or develop fully."

Throughout our lives, we come of age, as our inner selves are continuously challenged by the outer world. Life holds many tests, and we cannot predict what they will be, or how we will respond to them.

The time of life when *coming of age* is most evident are those years when we cross the bridge from childhood to adulthood. The events that occur during that period, and the decisions that we make in reaction to them, often determine who we will become and how our lives will unfold.

The term *coming of age* has long been used in reference to stories that have a young character who, by the end of the story, has been tested and has grown in some way, as a result of some trial or hardship to which they have been forced to respond.

In *Come of Age*, young Timothy must let go of a strong love and a treasured fantasy. How can he grasp such a terrible loss? His loss seems even more frightening when it threatens his understanding of *who* his parents are and what makes his family whole. He will go on with life, one day at a time, doing the best he can.

B. J. Chute
Come of Age

Timothy crossed the road at the exact place where the tar ended and the dirt began, paused on the sidewalk, squinted up at the sun and gave a heave of satisfaction. He was too warm with his sweater on. He had known he was going to be too warm, and he had made a firm announcement to this effect to his mother before he left the house in the morning. Thousands of layers of woolly stuff, he had pointed out darkly, intimating[1] that a person might easily suffocate.

Having barely survived this fate so far, he now decided to make a test case out of it. If an automobile passed him on the road before he had counted up to ten, that meant it was really spring and too warm for sweaters. His own internal workings were positive on the subject, but he was amiably[2] willing to put the whole thing on a sporting basis.

"One," said Timothy. After a while, he added, "Two." He then suspended his counting while he made a neat pile of his schoolbooks and lunch box, putting them carefully on a bare patch of ground, away from the few greenly white sprigs of grass that were struggling up into the sunlight. If the car came by, he would have to put the books on the ground anyhow, in order to take off his sweater, so it seemed wiser to do it ahead of time.

"Three," said Timothy, looking up the road. There was nothing in sight, so he closed his eyes, waited, said "Four" and opened them again.

---

1. *intimating* (IN tih MAY ting): hinting
2. *amiably* (AY mee ub LEE): good-naturedly; agreeably

This time it worked. There was a car coming. Timothy put his hands to his sweater and stood pantingly prepared to jerk it over his head.

The car swished by with a friendly toot.

"Five-six-seven-eight-nine-ten," said Timothy rapidly, just to be perfectly fair about the whole thing, vanished momentarily into the sweater and reappeared with his hair standing on end and the expression of one who had been saved from total collapse in the nick of time.

He turned his sweater virtuously right side up again, with his mother in mind, and tied its arms around his waist, allowing the rest of it to fall comfortably to the rear where it could flap without giving him any sense of responsibility. Then he tucked his schoolbooks under one arm, picked up the lunch box and peered hopefully inside it. There were three cake crumbs and some orange peel. He licked his finger, collected the crumbs on the end of it and disposed of them tidily, then extracted a piece of the peel and took a thoughtful nibble.

It tasted rather leathery so he put it back, felt a momentary dejection based on a sudden desperate need for a great deal of food, recovered rapidly, took another look at the sun and gave a pleased snort.

It was certainly spring, and for once it was starting on a Friday afternoon, which meant he would have the whole weekend to get used to it in. Also, by some great and good accident, his sixth-grade English teacher had forgotten to assign the weekly composition. This was most incredibly gratifying, especially since the rumor had got around that she had been going to give them the dismal topic of What My Country Means to Me.

Timothy sighed with satisfaction over the narrow escape of the sixth-grade English class, knowing quite well the same topic would turn up again next week, but that next week was years away. Besides, she might change her mind and assign something else. One week she had told them to write what she referred to as a word portrait, called A Member of My Family. Timothy had enjoyed that one richly. He had written, inevitably, about his brother Bricky, and it was the longest composition he had ever achieved in his life. He felt a great pity for his classmates, who didn't have Bricky to write about, since Bricky was not only the most remarkable person in the world but he was also magnificently engaged in fighting the Japanese in the South Pacific. He was an Air Force pilot with silver wings and a bomber, and Timothy basked luxuriously in the warmth of his glory.

"Yoicks," said Timothy, addressing the spring and life in general. *Yoicks* was Bricky's favorite expression.

"Yoicks," he said again.

He was, at that moment, five blocks from home. The first block he used up in not stepping on the cracks in the sidewalk, which was not the mindless process it appeared to be. He was actually conducting an elaborate reconnaissance program,[3] and the cracks were vital supply lines. By the second block, however, his attitude on supplies had taken a more personal turn, and he spent the distance reflecting that this was the day his mother baked cookies. His imagination carried him willingly up the back steps, through the unlatched screen door and to the cooky jar, but there it gave up for lack of specific information on the type of cookies involved.

Besides, he was now at the third block, and the third block was important, consisting largely of a vacant lot with a run-down little shack lurching sideways in a corner of it. The old brown grass of last autumn and the matted tangle of vines and weeds were showing a faint stirring of greenness like a pale web.

At the edge of the lot, Timothy paused and his whole manner changed. He became alert and his eyes narrowed, shifting from left to right. He was listening intently. The only sound was the peevish chirp of a sparrow, but Timothy was a world away from it. What he was listening for was the warning roar of revved-up motors.

In a moment now, from behind that shack, from beyond those tangled vines, Japanese planes would swarm upward viciously, in squadron attack.

Timothy put down the books and the lunch box, then he stepped back, holding himself steady. His hand moved, fingers curved knowingly, to control and throttle,[4] and from his parted lips there suddenly burst a chattering roar.

---

3. *reconnaissance* (rih KAHN uh suntz) *program*: a general survey of an enemy's territory, to be followed by a more detailed spying mission

4. *throttle* (THRAHT uhl): the valve that controls the flow of fuel into the engine

The Liberator surged forward gallantly to meet the attackers. Timothy's face became tense, and he interrupted the engine's explosive revolutions for a moment to warn himself grimly, "This is it. Watch yourselves, men." He then nodded soberly. It was a grave responsibility for the pilot, knowing the crew trusted him to see them through.

The pilot, of course, was Bricky. It was Bricky who was holding the plane steady on its course, nerving himself for the final instant of action. The deadly swarm of Zeros swept forward, but the pilot's face remained impassive.

Z-z-z-zoom, they spread across the sky, their evil advance punctuated by the hail of machine-gun fire. The Liberator climbed, settling back on her tail in instant response to the pilot's sure hand. As she scaled the clouds, the bright silver of her name, painted along the side, shone defiantly—The Hornet. Bricky had at one time piloted a plane called The Hornet. It was the best name that Timothy knew.

After that, it was short and sharp. A Japanese fighter detached himself from the humming swarm. The Hornet rolled and the tail gunner squeezed the triggers. The plane exploded in midair, disintegrated and streamered[5] to earth in flaming wreckage.

"Right on the nose," said the gunner with satisfaction.

The Hornet had their range now. Zero after Zero fluttered helplessly down out of the sky, dissolving into the earth. The others turned and skittered for their home base, terrified before the invincibility[6] of American man and machine.

A faint smile flickered across the face of The Hornet's pilot, and he permitted himself a nod. "Good show," he said.

Timothy sat down on the ground and drew a deep breath. Then he said "Gosh!" and scrambled back to his feet. At home, even now, there might be a letter waiting from Bricky, full of breathless and wonderful details that could be relayed to the fellows at school. A few of them, of course, had brothers of their own in the Air Force, but none of them had

---

5. *streamered* (STREEM erd): fell to earth in long, wavy pieces resembling "streamers"
6. *invincibility* (in VINTS ih BILL ih TEE): the quality of being impossible to defeat

Bricky, and that made all the difference. He was quite sorry for them, but most willing to share and to expound.[7]

Gosh, he missed Bricky, but, gosh, it was worth it.

A dream crept across his mind. Maybe the war would last for years. Maybe some one of these days, a new pilot would stand before his commanding officer somewhere in Pacific territory and make a firm salute. "Lieutenant Baker reporting for duty, sir."

His commanding officer would look up quickly from his notes. "Timothy!" Bricky would say, holding it all back. They would shake hands.

For the entire next block toward home, Timothy shook hands with his brother, but on the last block spring got into his heels and he raced the distance like a lunatic, yelling his jubilee. The porch steps he took in two leaps, crashed happily into the front hall and smacked his books and his lunch box down on the hall table. He then opened his mouth to shout for his mother, not because he wanted her for anything specific but because he simply needed to know her exact location.

His mouth, opened to "Hey, mom!" closed suddenly in surprise. His father's hat was lying on the hall table. There was nothing to prepare him for his father's hat on the hall table at three-thirty in the afternoon. His father's hat kept regular hours. An unaccountable sense of formality descended on Timothy. He looked anxiously into the hall mirror and made a gesture toward flattening the top lock of his hair. It sprang up again under his hand, and he compromised on untying the sleeves of his sweater from around his waist and putting it firmly down on top of his books. None of this had anything to do with his father, who maintained strict neutrality on the subject of his son's appearance. It was entirely a matter between Timothy, the time of day, and that unexpected gray felt hat on the hall table.

There were a dozen reasons for his father's having come home early. There was nothing to get excited about. Timothy turned his back on the hall table and went through into the living room. There was no one there,

---

7. *expound* (ex POUND): explain in detail

but he could hear his father's voice in the kitchen, and, because the kitchen was a reassuring place, he felt better. He went on into the kitchen, shoving the door only partly open and easing himself through it.

His mother was sitting on the kitchen chair beside the kitchen table. She was just sitting there, not doing anything. She never sat anywhere like that, doing nothing.

The formal pressed-down feeling returned to Timothy and stuck in his throat.

He looked toward his father appealingly, but his father was leaning against the sink, with his hands behind him pressed against it, and staring down at the floor.

"Mom—" said Timothy.

They both looked at him then, but it was his father who answered. He answered right away, as if it had to be said very fast. "You'll have to know, Tim," he said, almost roughly. "It's Bricky. He's missing in action."

Missing in action. He had met the phrase so many times that it wasn't frightening. There was no possible connection in his mind between "Missing in action" and Bricky... Missing in action. Bricky, the invincible, would have bailed out, perhaps somewhere in the jungle. Or he would have nursed his damaged crate down to earth in a fantastically cool exhibition of flying skill, his men trusting him to see them through.

A hot, fierce pride surged up in Timothy. He wanted to tell his mother and father not to look that way, to tell them that Bricky, wherever he was, was safe. He wanted to reassure them, so they would be smiling at him again and all the old cozy confidence would return to the kitchen.

His father was dragging words out, one by one. "The plane didn't come back," he said. "They were on a bombing mission, and they didn't come back. We just got the telegram."

An awful thing happened then. Timothy's mother began to cry. He had never in his life seen her cry. It had never occurred to him that she was capable of it, and a monstrous chasm[8] of insecurity yawned suddenly at his feet.

---

8. *chasm* (KAZM): a huge hole in the earth

Timothy stood there in the middle of the floor with his hands jammed stiffly into his pockets and his eyes turned away from his father and mother. He was much more frightened by their sudden unfamiliarity than by what his father had told him. "Missing in action" was just words. His mother crying was a sheer impossibility, made visible before him.

He realized that he had to get out of the kitchen right away, because it was the place where had had always been safest, and now that made it unendurable. He couldn't do anything, anyway. Later, when his mother wasn't—when his mother felt better, he could explain to her about Bricky being all right. He slid out of the room like a ghost, and, linked in their fear, neither of them even looked up.

In the front hall, he stopped for a moment. The spring sun outside was shining, bright and warm, on the street, and he knew exactly how the heat of it would feel slanting across his shoulders. But his mother had thought he ought to wear his sweater today. He wanted very badly to do something to make her feel better. He frowned and pulled the sweater on over his head, jamming his arms into the sleeves and resisting the temptation to push up the cuffs. It stretched them, his mother said.

He went slowly down the front steps, worrying about his mother. The words "missing in action" still meant exactly nothing to him. They were only another installment in the exciting war serial that was Bricky's Pacific adventures, and there was not the slightest shadow of doubt in his mind about Bricky's safe return, though he was eager for details. He guessed none of the other fellows at school had members of their family gallantly missing in action.

No, it wasn't Bricky that made him feel funny in the pit of his stomach. The thing was he hadn't known that grown-ups cried, and the discovery took a good deal of the stability out of his world.

His mother might go on being frightened for days ahead, until they heard that Bricky was all right, and he would be tiptoeing around her in his mind all the time to make things better for her, and what he would really be wanting would be for things to be again the way they had been before.

He didn't want to feel all unsettled inside. The way he felt now was the way he had felt the time they had been waiting to hear from his sister in California when the baby came. He had known quite well that Margaret would be fine and everything, but, just the same, the baby's coming had got into the house and filled it with uncertainties. Now it was the War Department. He was suddenly quite angry with the War Department. Bricky wasn't going to like it either, when he got back. He wouldn't like having his mother worried.

Timothy wished now he had stayed a little longer in the kitchen and asked a few questions. He would have liked to know what that War Department had said, and, as he went down the street without any particular aim or direction, he turned it over and over in his mind.

He had walked back, without meaning to, to the vacant lot with the old shack on it, and it occurred to him that, while he had been shooting down those planes in Bricky's Hornet, his mother and father had been there in the kitchen. Looking like that.

He left the sidewalk and walked into the grassy tangle, scuffing his shoes through last autumn's leaves. He would have liked some company, and he toyed for a moment with going over to Davy Peters' house and telling him that the War Department had sent them a telegram about Bricky, but decided against it.

He sat down on the grass with his back against the wall of the shack. He could feel the rough coolness of the brown boards even through his sweater, and the sun spilled warmth down his front. It was unthinkable that the shack should ever be more comfortable than the kitchen at home, but this time it was.

He wished he knew just what the telegram had said. There was something, he thought, that they always put in. Something about "We regret to inform you," but maybe that was just for soldiers' families when the soldier had gotten killed. He had read a story with that in it once, and it had made quite an impression, because in the story it was all tied up with not talking about the things you knew, and for days Timothy had gone around with a tightly shut mouth and the look of one who is giving no aid and comfort to the enemy. He had even torn the corners of all

Bricky's letters and burned them up with a fine secret feeling of citizenship, and then he had regretted it afterwards, when he remembered it was only the United States APO[9] address and no good to anyone. It was too bad, in a way, because they would have made a good collection. On the other hand, he already had eighteen separate and distinct collections, and the shelf in his room, the corner of the second drawer down in the living-room desk, and the excellent location behind the laundry tub in the basement were all getting seriously overcrowded.

He wondered if maybe later he could have the telegram. He could start a good collection with the telegram, he thought. He would print on a piece of paper, "Things Relating to My Brother Bricky," and paste it onto a box. He even knew the box he would use. It held his father's golf shoes, but some kind of arrangement could be worked out for putting the shoes somewhere else. His father was very good about that sort of thing, once he understood boxes were really needed, and, later on, this one could hold all the souvenirs and medals and things Bricky would bring home.

The telegram, which maybe began "We regret to inform you," would fit neatly into the box without having to be folded. It would go on with something about "your son, Lieutenant Ronald Baker," and then there would be something more, not quite clear in his mind, about "He is reported missing in action over the South Pacific, having failed to return from an important bombing mission."

Timothy scowled at a sparrow. There was another part that went with the "missing in action" part. Missing, believed—Missing, believed killed.

That was when it hit him. That was the moment when he suddenly realized what had happened, when the thing that the telegram stood for took shape clearly before him, not as something that had frightened his mother, but as something real about Bricky.

Bricky, his brother. Bricky, with whom he had sat a hundred times in this exact place and talked and talked, Bricky who went fishing with him, who showed him how to tie a sheepshank,[10] who was going to help him build a radio when he came back.

---

9. *APO*: Army Post Office
10. *sheepshank*: a kind of knot made on a rope to shorten it temporarily

"When he comes back," said Timothy aloud, licking his lips because they had unaccountably gone dry. But suppose now Bricky didn't come back? Suppose that telegram was the end of everything?

It was the vacant lot and the shack that weren't safe any more. In the kitchen, he had known, without questioning it, that Bricky was all right. It was here, out in the open, that fear had come crawling. Bricky was dead. He knew Bricky was dead, and he was dead thousands of miles from anywhere, and they wouldn't see him again ever.

Timothy sat there, and the pain in his stomach wasn't anything like the pain you got from eating too much or being hungry. He rocked back and forth, not very much, but enough to cradle the sharpness of it, being careful not to breathe, because if he breathed it went down too far inside and hurt too much. If he could just sit there, maybe, not breathing—

He couldn't. There came a time when his lungs took a deep gulp of air without his having anything to do with it, and when that time came there was no way of holding out any longer.

Bricky was dead. He gave a great strangled sob and rolled over on his face, sprawling across the ground, and everything that was good and safe and beautiful quit the earth and left him with nothing to hold on to. He clung to the grass, shaking desperately with fear and pain and loss, and the immensity and the loneliness and the danger of being a human rolled over and over him in drowning waves.

Behind him, the shack, which only a little while ago had been a shelter for the sneak attack of Zero planes, was immobile and solid in the sunshine. It was only a shack in a vacant lot. The tumbled weeds and vines above which The Hornet had swooped and soared were weeds and vines, not a battleground for airborne knights.

It wasn't that way. It wasn't that way at all. It had nothing to do with a gallant plane, outnumbered but triumphant. It had nothing to do with the Bricky who had flown in his brother's dreams—safe and invincible.

A plane was a thing that could be shot down out of the safe sky by murderous gunfire. Bricky was a man whose body could be thrown from the cockpit and spin senselessly down into cold water. It was a cheat. The whole thing was a cheat.

The war—this vague big thing that moved in shadowy headlines, in a glorious pageantry of medals and flags and brave men shaking hands—wasn't that at all. He had thought it was something like King Arthur and the Knights of the Round Table, that it shone with beauty and was very high and proud.

And it wasn't. It was fear and this hollowed panic inside him, and it was not seeing Bricky again. Not seeing him again ever.

That was why his mother had cried. That was why his father's voice had been so rough and quick. And it wasn't to be endured. He breathed in shivering gasps, there with his face buried in cool-smelling grass and earth and the sun friendly and gentle on his shoulders that didn't feel it any more. It would go on like this, day after day and week after week. Bricky was dead, and the place where Bricky had been would never be filled in.

That was what war was, and he knew about it now, and the knowledge was too awful and too immense to be borne. He wanted his mother. He wanted to run to her and to hold to her tightly and to cry his heart out with her arms around his shoulders and her reassuring voice in his ears.

But his mother felt like this, too, and his father. There was no safety anywhere. No one could help him, except himself, and he was eleven years old. He didn't want to know about all these things. He didn't want to know what war really was. He wanted it to be a story in a book, with excitement and glory and men being brave. Not this immense, unendurable fear and emptiness. He couldn't even cry.

He was eleven years old, and he lay there face down in the grass, and he couldn't cry. He groped for anything to ease him, and he thought perhaps Bricky's plane hadn't been alone when it crashed to the flat blue water. He thought that other planes might have been blotted out with it—planes with big red suns[11] painted on them.

But even that didn't do any good. There were men in those planes with the suns on them. Not men like men he knew, not Americans, but real people just the same. No one had told him that he would one day know

---

11. *big red suns*: Japan's national symbol during World War II

that the enemy were real people, no one had warned him against finding it out.

He pressed closer against the ground, trying to draw comfort up from it, but he kept shaking. It was a long, long time before the shaking stopped. He was surprised, at the end of it, to find that he was still there on the ground. He pushed away from it and sat up, his head swimming. The sun was much lower now, and a little wind had sprung up to move the vines around him so they swayed against the shack. The sweater felt good around his shoulders, and it was the sweater that made him realize suddenly that he couldn't go on lying there waiting for the world to stop and end the pain.

The world wasn't going to stop. It was going right on, and Timothy Baker was still in it. He would go on being in it, and the thing inside him would go on being the thing inside him. He would have, somehow, to live with that too. He would have to go back to the house, to his mother and father, to school, to coming home and knowing that Bricky wouldn't be there.

Timothy looked around. He felt weak and dizzy, the way he'd felt once after a fever. The shack was there, with no Zeros behind it. The place where he had stood when he was being Bricky and The Hornet was just a piece of ground. His mouth drew in, with his teeth clipping his lower lip, while he stared. There wasn't any escape. He would have to go back—along the sidewalk, up the path, through the front door, into the hallway, into the living room, into the kitchen. There wasn't any escape from his mother's eyes or his father's voice. He knew all about it now, and he was stiff and sore from knowing about it.

He saw what he had to do. He had to go home and face that telegram. He got to his feet. He brushed off the dry bits of grass that clung to the blurred wool of his sweater, and he pulled the cuffs around straight so they wouldn't be stretched wrong. Then he walked across the grass, out of the lot and onto the sidewalk, holding himself very carefully against the pain.

He held himself that way all the distance back, and when he got to his own front yard he was able to walk quite directly and quickly up the path and up the steps. He turned the doorknob, and he went into the front hall. It was getting darker outdoors already, and the hall was dim. It was a moment before he realized that his father was standing in the hallway, waiting for him.

He stopped where he was, getting the pieces of himself together. He wasn't even shaking now, and some vague kind of pride stirred deep down inside him.

He said "Dad—" dragging the monosyllable out.

"Yes, Timmy."

"May I see the telegram, please?"

His father reached into his pocket and took out the brown leather wallet that he carried papers around in. The telegram was on top of some letters and bills, and it was strange to see it already so much a part of their living that it was jostled by business things.

Timothy took the yellow envelope and opened it carefully. There it was. "Lieutenant Ronald Baker, missing in action." The stiff formality of the printed words made it seem so final that he felt the coldness and the fear spreading through him again, the way it had been at the shack. His mind wanted to drag away from the piece of paper, and he had to force it to think instead.

With careful stubbornness, he read the telegram again. It wasn't really very much that the War Department said—just that the plane had not returned and that the family would be advised of any further news. He read the last part once more. Any further news. That meant the War Department wasn't sure what had happened. Bricky might have bailed out somewhere. There had been stories in the newspaper about fliers who bailed out and were picked up later.

That was a hope. Timothy weighed it carefully in his mind, not letting himself clutch at it, and it was still a hope. It was a perfectly fair one that they were entitled to, he and his father and mother.

He held his thoughts steady on that for a moment, and then he made them go on logically and precisely. Another thing that could have happened was that Bricky had gone down somewhere over land that was held by the Japanese. If that was it, Bricky might be a prisoner of war.

Prisoners of war came back. That was another hope, and it was a perfectly fair one too.

He had two hopes, then. They were reasonable hopes, and he had a right to hang on to them very tightly. The telegram didn't say "believed killed."

Frowning, he went through it in his head again, adding up as if it were an arithmetic problem. There were three things that the telegram could mean. Two of them were on the side of Bricky's safety, and one was against it. Two chances to one was almost a promise.

Timothy drew a deep breath and handed the telegram back to his father. His father took it without saying anything, then he put his hand against the back of Timothy's neck and rubbed his fingers up through the stubbly hair. For just a moment, Timothy turned his head, pressing close against the buttons of his father's coat, then he pulled away.

"Can I go outdoors for a little while?" he said.

"Sure. I guess supper will be the usual time."

They nodded to each other, then Timothy turned and went out of the house. He went down the steps, his hands jammed in his pockets, and began to walk along the sidewalk, feeling still a little hollow, but perfectly steady.

His heart fitted him again. It had stopped pounding against the cage of his ribs, and it didn't hurt any more. The old feeling of safety and comfort was beginning to come back, but now it wasn't a part of his home or of the day. It was inside himself and solid, so that he couldn't mislay it again ever. He pushed his hair away from his forehead, letting the wind get at it. The air was cooler now and felt good, and he had a vague moment of being hungry.

Then he looked around him. He was back at the vacant shack, and the shack had been waiting there for him to come. He eyed it gravely. Behind the shack were the Zeros. They had been waiting for him too. He knew they were there and that their force was overwhelming. Timothy's fingers reached automatically for the controls of his plane. His jaw tightened and his eyes narrowed, and he opened his mouth to let out the roar of the motors.

And, suddenly, he stopped. His hand dropped down to his side and his mouth shut. He stood there quietly for a moment, as if he had lost something and was trying to remember what it was. Then he gave a sigh of relinquishment.[12]

His fingers curled firmly around air again and closed, but this time they didn't close on the controls of a machine. They closed on dangling reins.

"Come on, Silver, old boy," said Timothy softly to the evening. "They've got the jump on us, but we can catch them yet."

He touched his spurs to his gallant pinto pony, and wheeling, he loped away across the sunlit plain.

---

12. *relinquishment* (rih LINK wish MENT): letting go

Thinking It Over

1. Early in the story, Timothy develops a test for determining whether it is too warm for him to wear his sweater: If a car passes him before he counts to ten, he can remove it—which is the result he hopes for. Have you ever devised such a test for yourself? Describe a similar challenge you may have thought of, or make one up.

2. What do you think of the way that *Come of Age* is written? Is Timothy's grief described well? Is his coming to terms with his brother's probable death realistically handled? In your response, you may also consider whether you find Timothy's return to fantasy, in the final three paragraphs, believable. Moreover, are his interactions with his parents what you would expect? Please answer in four or five detailed paragraphs. If you have other points regarding the story that you wish to discuss, please include them.

3. The author writes that Timothy's teacher had forgotten to assign the weekly composition. What relevance does it have for the story that the topic was going to have been What My Country Means to Me?

4. As Timothy watches his parents together in the kitchen, what is his most immediate experience of loss?

5. Imagine that a second telegram arrives the next day. What do you think it will say?

Consider This...

Science fiction takes as many forms as there are types of fiction: Stories may be filled with drama or adventure or humor or the ordinary events of life. As with most other fiction, the foundation of good science fiction is skillful writing and a powerful message or theme.

Here we have a short science fiction tale set in modern times. In fact, the flaws and pressures of modern times are precisely the point. The protagonist goes off looking for the Acme Travel Agency, where a very special one-way voyage is rumored to be offered. Our hero, Charley Ewell, is selected for a ticket. What qualities does the travel agent see in Charley? Are these the same qualities that bring about the event at the end of the story?

When you have read the story, ask yourself whether Charley is typical of most people. Ask yourself where, given the choice that Charley was given, you would choose to live.

Jack Finney

Of Missing Persons

Walk in as though it were an ordinary travel agency. That's what the stranger I'd met at a party told me. Ask a few ordinary questions about a vacation or something. Then hint about The Folder. But whatever you do, don't mention it straight out. Wait till he brings it up. If he doesn't, you might as well forget it. If you can. Because you'll never see it. You're not the type, that's all. He'll just look at you as though he doesn't know what you're talking about.

I went over it all in my mind, again and again. But what seems possible at midnight at a party isn't easy to believe on a raw, rainy day. I felt like a fool, searching the store fronts for the street number. It was noon, West 42nd Street, New York. I walked with my head bent into the slanting rain. This was hopeless.

Anyway, I thought, who am I to see The Folder, even if there is one? Charley Ewell, a young guy who works in a bank. A teller. I don't like the job. I don't make much money, and I never will. I've lived here for over three years and haven't many friends. I see too many shows, and I'm sick of meals alone in diners. I have ordinary abilities, looks, and thoughts. Do I qualify?

Now I saw it, the address in the 200 block, an old office building. I pushed into the dirty lobby. The name was second on the list. "Acme[1] Travel Agency" between "A-1 Copy Shop" and "Ajax Magic Supplies." I

---

1. *Acme* (AK mee): the peak; the highest point

pressed the bell for the rickety elevator. I almost turned and left—this was crazy.

But upstairs, the Acme office was bright and clean. Behind a counter stood a tall man with a dignified look. He nodded at me to come in. My heart was pumping—he fitted the description exactly.

"Yes, United Air Lines," he was saying into the phone. "Flight"—he glanced at a paper—"seven-oh-three. I suggest you get there forty minutes early."

I waited, leaning on the counter, looking around. He was the man, all right. Yet this was just an ordinary travel agency. Big bright posters on the walls. Racks full of folders. Again I felt like a fool.

"Can I help you?" he said.

"Yes." Suddenly I was terribly nervous. "I'd like to—get away," I said. You fool, that's too fast, I told myself. Don't rush it! I watched in a kind of panic, but he didn't flick an eyelash.

"Well, there are a lot of places to go," he said politely. He brought out a folder: "Fly to Buenos Aires[2]—Another World!"

I looked at it long enough to be polite. Then I just shook my head. I was afraid to talk, afraid I'd say the wrong thing.

"Something quieter, maybe?" He brought out another folder: "The Unspoiled Forests of Maine." "Or"—he laid a third folder on the counter—"Bermuda[3] is nice just now."

I decided to risk it. "No," I said. "What I'm really looking for is a new place to live." I stared right into his eyes. "For the rest of my life." Then my nerve failed me,[4] and I tried to think of a way to get out of it.

But he only smiled and said, "I don't know why we can't advise you on that." He leaned forward. "What are you looking for? What do you want?"

I held my breath, then said it. "Escape."

"From what?"

"Well—" Now I wasn't sure. I'd never put it into words before. "From New York, I'd say. And all cities. From worry. And fear. And the things I

2. *Buenos Aires* (BWAY nus I riz): the capital city of Argentina
3. *Bermuda* (ber MYOO duh): a popular vacation spot—a group of islands in the Atlantic
4. *my nerve failed me*: I lost my courage

read in my newspapers. From loneliness." And then I couldn't stop, though I knew I was talking too much. "From never doing what I really want to do or having much fun. From selling my days just to stay alive." I looked straight at him and said softly. "From the world."

Now he was studying my face, staring at me. I knew that in a moment he'd shake his head. "Mister," he'd say, "you better get to a doctor." But he didn't. He kept staring. He was a big man, his lined face very intelligent, very kind. He looked the way ministers should look. He looked the way all fathers should look.

He lowered his gaze. I had the sudden idea that he was learning a great deal about me. More than I knew about myself. Suddenly he smiled. "Do you like people?" he asked. "Tell the truth. I'll know if you aren't."

"Yes. It isn't easy for me to relax, though, and be myself, and make friends."

He nodded. "Would you say you're a pretty decent kind of man?"

"I guess so. I think so." I shrugged.

"Why?"

This was hard to answer. "Well—at least when I'm not, I'm usually sorry about it."

He grinned. "You know," he said casually, "we sometimes get people in here who seem to be looking for pretty much what you are. So just as a sort of little joke—"

I couldn't breathe. This was what I'd been told he would say if he thought I might do.

"—we've had a little folder printed. Simply for our own amusement, you understand. And for a few customers like you. So I'll have to ask you to look at it here, if you're interested."

I could barely whisper, "I'm interested."

He brought out a long, thin folder, the same size and shape as the others. He slid it over the counter toward me.

I looked at it, pulling it closer with a fingertip—I was almost afraid to touch it. The cover was dark blue, the shade of a night sky. Across the top in white letters it said, "Visit Enchanting Verna!"[5] The cover was sprinkled with stars. In the lower left was a globe, the world, with clouds around it. At the upper right, just under the word "Verna" was a star larger and brighter than the others. Across the bottom it said, "Peaceful Verna, where life is the way it *should* be."

Inside were pictures, so beautiful they looked real. In one picture you could see dew shining on the grass, and it looked wet. In another, a tree trunk seemed to curve out of the page. It was a shock to touch it and feel paper instead of bark. Tiny human faces, in a third picture, seemed about to speak.

I studied a large picture taken from the top of a hill. The valley was covered with forest. Curving through it, far below, ran a stream, blue as the sky with spots of foaming white. It seemed that if you'd only look closely, you'd be sure to see that stream move. In clearings beside the stream were rough cabins. Under the picture were the words, "The Colony."

"Fun fooling around with a thing like that," the man said. "Eases the boredom. Nice-looking place, isn't it?"

I could only nod, staring at that forest-covered valley. This was how America must have looked when it was new. And you knew this was only a part of a whole land of unspoiled forests, where every stream ran pure.

Under that picture was another, of six or eight people on a beach. They were sitting, kneeling, or squatting in an easy way. It was morning, just after breakfast. They were smiling, one woman talking, the others listening. One man had half risen to skip a stone out onto the surface of the water.

You knew this: that they were spending twenty minutes or so down on that beach after breakfast before going to work. You knew they were friends, and that they did this every day. You knew—I tell you, you *knew*—that they liked their work, all of them, whatever it was. I'd never seen anything like their faces before. They were ordinary enough in looks. But these people were *happy*. Even more, you knew they'd *been* happy,

---

5. *Verna* (VUR nuh): the word *vernal* means something that occurs in the springtime or something that suggests springtime or youth; the author is hinting that in this place, one feels young, and the season is always spring

day after day, for a long time. And that they always would be, and they knew it.

I wanted to join them. I *longed* to. And I could hardly stand it. I looked up at the man, and tried to smile. "This is—very interesting," I said.

"Yes." He smiled back. "We've had people so interested, so carried away, that they didn't want to talk about anything else." He laughed. "They actually wanted to know prices, details, everything."

I nodded. "And I suppose you've worked out a whole story to go with the folder?" I said.

"Oh, yes. What would you like to know?"

"These people," I said softly, touching the picture of the group on the beach. "What do they do?"

"They work. Everyone does." He took a pipe from his pocket. "Some study. Some of our people farm, some write, some make things with their hands. Most of them raise children, and—well, they work at whatever it is they really want to do."

"And if there isn't anything they really want to do?"

He shook his head. "There's always something for everyone. It's just that here, we so rarely have time to find out what it is." He looked at me gravely.[6] "Life is simple there, and it's serene.[7] In some ways, the good ways, it's like the life of early American pioneers. But without the drudgery[8] that killed people young. We have electricity, washing machines, vacuum cleaners, modern bathrooms, and modern medicine.

"But there are no radios, telephones, or cars. People live and work in small villages. They raise or make most of the things they use. They build their own houses, with all the help they need from their neighbors. They have a lot of fun, but there's nothing you buy a ticket to. They have shows, card parties, weddings, birthdays, harvest parties, swimming, and sports of all kinds. People talk with each other a lot, and visit, and share meals. There are no pressures. Life holds few threats. Everyone is happy." After a moment, he smiled. "That's how the story goes in our little joke," he said, nodding at the folder.

---

6. *gravely*: seriously
7. *serene* (suh REEN): peaceful and calm
8. *drudgery* (DRUJ uh ree): hard, boring work

"Who are you?" I lifted my eyes from the folder to look at him.

"It's in the folder," he said. "The people of Verna—the original ones—are just like you. Verna is a planet of air, sun, land, and sea, like Earth. The weather's about the same. There are a few small bodily differences between you and us—but nothing important. We read and enjoy your books. We like your chocolate, which we didn't have, and your music. But our thoughts, and aims, and history—those have been very different from Earth's." He smiled. "Amusing fantasy,[9] isn't it?"

"Yes." I knew I sounded abrupt. "And where is Verna?"

"Light years away, by your measurements."

I was suddenly annoyed. I didn't know why. "A little hard to get to then, wouldn't it be?"

He turned to the window beside him. "Come here," he said, and I walked around the counter to stand beside him. "There, off to the left, are two apartment buildings, built back to back. See them?"

I nodded, and he said, "A man and his wife live on the fourteenth floor of one of those buildings. A wall of their living room is the back wall of the building. They have friends on the fourteenth floor of the other building. A wall of *their* living room is the back wall of *their* building. In other words, these two couples live within two feet of one another.

"But when the Robinsons want to visit the Braedens, they walk from their living room to the front door. Then they walk down a long hall to the elevators. They ride fourteen floors down. Then, in the street, they must walk around to the next block. And the city blocks there are long. In bad weather, they've sometimes actually taken a cab. They walk into the other building, then go on through the lobby. They ride up fourteen floors, walk down a hall, ring a bell, and finally go into their friends' living room—only two feet from their own."

He turned back to the counter, and I walked around to the other side again. "All I can tell you," he said, "is that the way the Robinsons travel is like space travel. But if they could only step through those two feet of wall—well, that's how we travel. We don't cross space, we avoid it." He smiled. "Draw a breath here—and exhale it on Verna."

---

9. *fantasy* (FAN tuh see): dream; something imagined

I said softly, "That's how they arrived, isn't it? The people in the picture. You took them there." He nodded, and I said, "Why?"

He shrugged. "If you saw a neighbor's house on fire, would you rescue his family if you could?"

"Yes."

"Well—so would we."

"You think it's that bad, then? With us?"

"How does it look to you?"

I thought about the headlines every morning. "Not so good."

He just nodded and said, "We can't take you all. We can't even take very many. So we've been choosing a few."

"For how long?"

"A long time." He smiled. "One of us was a member of Lincoln's cabinet."

I leaned across the counter toward him. "I like your little joke," I said. "I like it very much. When does it stop being a joke?"

For a moment, he studied me. Then he spoke. "Now, if you want it to."

You've got to decide on the spot, the man at the party had told me. *Because you'll never get another chance. I know. I've tried.*

Now I stood there thinking. There were people I'd hate never to see again. This was the world I'd been born in. Then I thought about going back to my job, back to my room at night. And finally I thought of the deep-green valley in the picture, and the beach.

"I'll go," I whispered. "If you'll have me."

He studied my face. "Be sure," he said sharply. "Be certain. We want no one there who won't be happy. If you have any least doubt, we'd prefer that—"

"I haven't."

After a moment, he slid open a drawer under the counter and brought out what looked like a railroad ticket. The printing said, "Good for ONE TRIP TO VERNA. Not transferable. One-way only."

"Ah—how much?" I said, reaching for my wallet.

"All you've got. Including your small change." He smiled.

"I don't have much."

"That doesn't matter. We once sold a ticket for $3,700. And we sold another just like it for six cents." He handed the ticket to me. On the back were the words, "Good this day only" and the date. I put $11.17 on the counter. "Take the ticket to the Acme Depot,"[10] he said. Leaning across the counter, he gave me directions.

It's a tiny hole-in-the-wall, the Acme Depot. You may have seen it. It's just a little store front on one of the narrow streets west of Broadway. Inside, there's a worn wooden counter and a few battered, chrome-and-plastic chairs. The man at the counter glanced up as I stepped in. He looked for my ticket. When I showed it, he nodded at the last empty chair. I sat down.

There was a girl beside me, hands folded on her purse. Rather young, she looked like a secretary. Across the way sat a young man in work clothes. His wife, beside him, was holding their little girl in her lap. And there was a man of around fifty. He was expensively dressed. He looked like the vice-president of a bank, I thought. I wondered what his ticket had cost.

Maybe twenty minutes passed. Then a small, battered old bus pulled up at the curb outside. The bus had dented fenders and tires with worn tread. It was just the sort of little bus you see around, ridden always by shabby, tired, silent people, going no one knows where.

It took nearly two hours for the little bus to work south through the traffic. We all sat, each wrapped in thought. We stared out the rain-splattered windows. I watched wet people huddled at city bus stops. I saw them rap angrily on the closed doors of full buses. At 14th Street I saw a speeding cab splash dirty water on a man at the curb. I saw the man's mouth twist as he cursed. I saw hundreds of faces, and not once did I see anyone smile.

I dozed. Then we were on a shiny black highway somewhere on Long Island. I slept again and woke up in darkness. I caught a glimpse of a farmhouse. Then the bus slowed, lurched once, and stopped. We were parked beside what looked like a barn.

---

10. *depot* (DEE poe): a railroad or bus station

It *was* a barn. The driver walked up to it. He pulled the big sliding door open and stood holding it as we filed in. Then he let it go, stepping inside with us. The big door slid closed of its own weight.

The barn smelled of cattle. There was nothing inside on the dirt floor but a bench of unpainted pine. The driver pointed to it with the beam of his flashlight. "Sit here, please," he said quietly. "Get your tickets ready." Then he moved down the line, punching tickets. His beam of light moved along the floor. I caught a glimpse of tiny piles of round bits of cardboard, like confetti. Then he was at the door again. He slid it open just enough to pass through. For a moment, we saw his outline against the night sky.

"Good luck," he said. "Just wait where you are." He let go of the door. It slid closed, snipping off the beam of his flashlight. A moment later, we heard the motor start and the bus lumber[11] away.

The dark barn was silent now, except for our breathing. Time ticked away. I felt an urge to speak. But I didn't quite know what to say. I began to feel embarrassed, a little foolish. I was very aware that I was simply sitting in an old barn. The seconds passed. I moved my feet restlessly. Soon I was getting cold.

Then suddenly I knew! My face blushed in violent anger and shame. We'd been tricked! We'd been swindled out of our money. How? By our pitiful desire to believe an absurd[12] fairy tale. Now we were left to sit there as long as we pleased. Finally, we'd come to our senses. Then we'd make our way home, like others before us, as best we could.

It was suddenly impossible to understand how I could have been so stupid. I was on my feet, stumbling in the dark across the uneven floor. I had some idea of getting to a phone and the police. The big barn door was heavier than I'd thought. But I slid it back and stepped through. Then I turned to shout back to the others to come along.

As I turned, the inside of that barn came alight. Through every wide crack of its walls and ceiling and windows streamed light. It was the light of a brilliantly blue sky. I opened my mouth to shout. Suddenly, the air was sweeter than any I had ever tasted. Then dimly, through a dusty

---

11. *lumber* (LUM ber): move clumsily or heavily
12. *absurd* (ub ZURD): ridiculous

window of that barn, I saw it. For less than the blink of an eye. I saw a deep, forest-covered valley, a blue stream winding through it, and a sunny beach. That picture was imprinted in my mind forever.

Then the heavy door slid shut. My fingernails scraped along the wood in a desperate effort to stop it. I failed. I was standing alone in a cold, rainy night.

It took four or five seconds, no longer, to get the door open again. But it was four or five seconds too long. The barn was empty, dark. There was nothing inside but a worn, pine bench. By the light of a match, I saw tiny drifts of what looked like confetti on the floor. I knew where everyone was. They were laughing out loud in that forest-green valley, and walking toward home.

I work in a bank, in a job I don't like. I ride to and from it in the subway, reading the daily news. I live in a rented room. In my battered dresser, under a pile of handkerchiefs, is a little square of yellow cardboard. Printed on its face are the words, "Good for ONE TRIP TO VERNA." Stamped on the back is a date. But the date is gone, long since.

I've been back to the Acme Travel Bureau. The tall man walked up to me and laid $11.17 on the counter. "You left this the last time you were here," he said. He looked me right in the eyes and added blankly. "I don't know why." Then some customers came in. He turned to greet them, and there was nothing for me to do but leave.

Walk in as though it were an ordinary travel bureau. You can find it, somewhere, in any city you try! Ask a few ordinary questions about a vacation, anything. Then hint about The Folder. But whatever you do, don't mention it straight out. Give him time to size you up and offer it. And if he does, if you can believe—then make up your mind and stick to it! Because you won't ever get a second chance. I know, because I've tried. And tried. And tried.

Thinking It Over

1. Why does Charley Ewell ask, Who am I to see the Folder?

2. How does Charley sum up his life at present?

3. Who are the missing persons of the title?

4. Why does Charley miss the trip?

5. Why would a person know about the travel agency, but still be here to tell the story?

Consider This...

What is it that we first see, when we begin a story? The *title*. Authors give quite a bit of thought to choosing or creating a title. When you have finished reading this story, ask yourself why it is called *The Gold Medal*. What is the significance of the gold medal? Why is it given?

As the story opens, you meet Amanda, a girl who is just about your age. You will follow her through a day that is full of struggles. Amanda seems to resent being challenged to do her best. For her, this means she is not being seen for who she really is—for herself. Why is Amanda, in fact, forced to try harder than other kids her age?

Amanda is a girl of intensity and stamina. In spite of her difficulties and her angry feelings, she seems like a person who won't give up and will work things out. Will she remain angry, or will she translate some of her resentment into accomplishment? Is her anger justified? As you read the story, see if you can see the events from more than one point of view.

Nan Gilbert

The Gold Medal

The day had been too much for Amanda. It had started out bad and got no better, one thing piling on another all day long.

"That skirt is too short," her mother had frowned during this morning's last-minute inspection. "Did you scrub your teeth? Are your fingernails clean?"

"Mom, I'm not a *baby*!" Amanda had let out a hopeless squawk and fled. It was no use. When her mother looked at her, she didn't see Amanda—not really. She saw an Example to help show their new neighbors that the Dawsons were as clean and quiet and well-mannered as any family on the block.

"I'm not an Example!" grumbled Amanda rebelliously.[1] "I'm *me*!"

Amanda Dawson—tall for her years, a little thin, leggy as a newborn colt. Flopping short black ponytail, jutting[2] elbows, springy knees. Long feet that could trip her up—and frequently did. Face plain and unremarkable except for large, liquid, chocolate-brown eyes, just one shade darker than her scrubbed, shining skin.

What did her mother see, if she didn't see Amanda? Amanda's quick imagination leaped to present her with the picture of a Proper Example: a spotlessly clean, tidy creature who kept her elbows in and her knees hidden...whose hair never worked loose from its tight rubberband...

---

1. *rebelliously* (rih BEL yuss lee): refusing to accept someone's authority
2. *jutting* (JUTT ing): sticking out

who didn't run or shout or use slang...whose name was always on the honor roll...

"You there—shoo! Don't trespass! Keep to the sidewalk!"

Absorbed[3] in her picture-making, Amanda had unthinkingly taken the shortcut across Mrs. Hawthorne's corner lot. Now the old lady had popped from her house like a cuckoo from a clock.

"Oh, woe!" muttered Amanda, retreating quickly. "Here we go again!"

The first time this had happened, Amanda had felt bewildered. The shortcut was worn bare by years of schoolchildren's feet, and others seemed to be using it freely.

"I'm not hurting anything," she had said.

Her protest roused the old lady to a flurry of shrill bird-like cries. "This is private property—I have my rights!"

Now, loping back to the sidewalk, pursued by indignant[4] chirps, Amanda told herself resignedly,[5] "Mrs. Hawthorne doesn't see me either." When the old lady looked at Amanda, it was as though she saw not just one girl, but a whole regiment[6] of Amandas, marching across her lot, crushing flowers and shrubs!

Amanda sighed. How did you make someone really *see* you? So they'd know you were *you*? Not a Regiment. Not an Example.

Not a Gang of Hoodlums, either! That's what Mr. Grogan always saw when he looked at her, Amanda decided. By the time Amanda entered Mr. Grogan's store to buy a candy bar, her imagination was growing livelier by the minute.

Mr. Grogan was all smiles and jokes—"Well, well, what's it going to be this time? A nice big box of chocolates, maybe?" he asked.

But he watched Amanda carefully as she lingered over the candy display. When she brought her purchase to the counter, he made an

---

3. *absorbed* (uhb ZORBD): engrossed; completely involved in

4. *indignant* (in DIG nunt): displeased by something considered unjust or insulting

5. *resignedly* (ree ZYN ud lee): giving up and accepting something one doesn't really want to accept

6. *regiment* (REJ ih ment): a unit of soldiers or a group of people who have all been taught to behave the same way

excuse to peek into her lunch sack—"My, my, won't get any fatter on a diet like that!"

No need to look—I didn't steal anything! For a second, Amanda was afraid she had said the words out loud. Mom would split a seam if she even suspected Amanda of speaking up like that, pert[7] and sassy! Hastily, Amanda grabbed her sack and ducked out of the store. Until she had her imagination under control, she'd better keep a close guard on her tongue!

Head down, Amanda scuffed slowly toward school. The day had hardly begun and already it rested heavily on her shoulders. Nor did she expect anything inside the walls of Jefferson School to lighten the load.

School was Amanda's greatest trial this fall. Instead of a familiar building filled with old friends, her family's move to a new home had made Amanda a stranger among strangers. As yet she had made no real friends to replace those she had lost. Though some of the girls were cordial[8] and kind, nobody asked her home after school or stopped at Amanda's house for cookies and pop. And she knew there were others—or maybe it was their parents—who didn't like her being at Jefferson at all. This thought added to the day's accumulating[9] weight of gloom.

During the noon break, Amanda avoided the lunchroom. She took her sack-lunch outside to a sheltered corner of the building. For some reason, today the sunny nook seemed lonely. Each bite Amanda swallowed had to fight its way past a great lump that unexpectedly blocked her throat.

When the bell summoned her back to class, Amanda reluctantly joined the hurrying, chattering crowds in the hall. Her next class was science, taught by Mr. Moore. Amanda thought Mr. Moore the nicest of all the teachers; for him she tried extra hard to do good work. Her first lonely, awkward day in Jefferson, Mr. Moore had welcomed her with genuine warmth. And he was always generous with after-school time, ready to help her if there was something she didn't understand.

---

7. *pert* (PURT): bold and impertinent; slightly disrespectful
8. *cordial* (KOR juhl): friendly and courteous
9. *accumulating* (uh KYOO myuh LAY ting): mounting; growing

But now, slumped low in her backrow seat, with the lump still big in her throat and a growing heaviness in her heart, Amanda thought, "He doesn't see me either. He'd treat *any* black kid the same way." Because he's kindhearted. Because he truly wants to help a black child fit into a white world. For him, she was the symbol of a cause he believed in. She wasn't herself at all.

Mr. Moore had to call her name twice before she realized he had asked her a question. Amanda stared at him somberly.[10]

"I don't know," she said.

"Oh, come now, Amanda, of course you do. Remember, it's what we talked about yesterday—"

"I don't know!" The lump in Amanda's throat broke suddenly into a loud, dismaying[11] sob. "Why is it so awful if *I* don't know? Lots of times *they* don't know, and you never look so—so—" It was Mr. Moore's look of hurt surprise that sent her dashing out of the room, that and the new and louder sob rising in her throat.

From the doorway she turned to face him. "I don't care—it's true!—I've got as much right to be st-stupid as anybody!" The second sob got away from her before she could slam the door. Humiliated, she pelted[12] down the hall and out of the building.

The day was too lovely for gloom—an Indian summer afternoon, with rich golden warmth spread over the fields and hills like eiderdown[13] quilt. In spite of herself, her bowed shoulders lifted, her heart lightened...

And she began to run. Running, to Amanda, was like flying. There was special joy in the clean rush of air against her upraised face, the pounding blood in her veins. When Amanda ran, she left all her coltish awkwardness behind. Her stride lengthened; her arms pumped; her long feet—that could trip her up when she walked—barely skimmed the ground.

Down the road she flew, and across a pasture where horses pricked their ears at her in mild amazement. She had to stop for breath— panting, laughing, giddy with this supercharge of oxygen—then she was off again.

---

10. *somberly* (SAHM bur lee): seriously and gloomily
11. *dismaying* (diss MAY ing): causing agitation and unhappiness
12. *pelted* (PELT ed): rushed
13. *eiderdown* (I dur down): soft duck feathers

Up and over a gentle slope where a giant cottonwood[14] offered an oasis of cool green shade she flew.

Too late Amanda saw the high heap of overturned earth below the tree. The springs in her tiring legs coiled and propelled her upward. Arms and legs stretched wide in a split. Thin body bent flat over her forward knee, Amanda cleared the pile of dirt—

But not the excavation[15] behind it. Arms flailing, legs treading the air, she lunged[16] for the far side, then fell back ingloriously[17] into the hole.

"You hurt?" a voice asked with quavery[18] concern.

Amanda sat up, dazed, and brushed dirt from her hands and skirt. Her startled brown eyes, almost level with the rim of hollowed-out earth, saw for the first time the bent figure of an old man under the tree.

"N-no," she said.

"That was mighty pretty running," the old man said with approval, "and as nice a hurdle[19] as ever I've seen. I'm glad you didn't hurt yourself." After a moment, he added, "That's a grave you're settin' in."

Amanda squeaked and scrambled out onto the grass. "A—a *grave*?"

"Yep, for Chief. Chief's my dog."

"Oh—" Amanda cast about for words. "I—I'm sorry he's dead."

"He isn't. Not yet anyway." The old man struggled to his feet. He leaned heavily on his spade as he surveyed his handiwork. "Just about ready. Yep, a few more days and it'll be done. Wouldn't want anyone else to dig it—not for Chief. But if I was to do it, I figured I'd better get started. Can't turn more'n a few spadefuls a day."

Amanda looked at the excavation over which the old man was now pulling a piece of tarpaulin.[20] "He—must be a big dog."

"He's that, all right. Used to be, anyway." The old man weighted the tarpaulin with a rock at each corner, then straightened slowly. "Kinda thin

---

14. *cottonwood* (KAHT un wood): a type of poplar tree that has cottony tufts on the seeds
15. *excavation* (EX kuh VAY shun): a hole that has been made by digging
16. *lunged* (LUNJD): moved forward suddenly
17. *ingloriously* (in GLOR ee us lee): simply and looking a bit foolish
18. *quavery* (KWAY vuh ree): shaky
19. *hurdle* (HUR dl): a leap
20. *tarpaulin* (TAR puh lin): a sheet of waterproof canvas

now, poor old boy. You want to come meet him? Chief was a runner, too, in his day—and his day lasted a lot longer than most."

Taking her consent for granted, he started down the other side of the slope toward a small house almost hidden behind a tangle of vines and shrubbery. Amanda looked a little wildly toward town, but an emotion much stronger than her alarm tugged her in the opposite direction. A runner, the old man had said—just like that. Here was someone who had looked at her and seen—not a Black Child or an Example or a Black Regiment, but Amanda herself—a runner. Wordless with upswelling gratitude, she followed the old man through a door. When Amanda's eyes adjusted to the dim light inside, she made out the form of a big black dog sprawled near the window in a dappling[21] of green-filtered sunlight. Except for a single thump of tail, he didn't move. The old man stooped low, patted the black head and scratched gently behind long velvety ears.

Cautiously, Amanda went nearer. She didn't know much about dogs; she was uncertain how to treat one that seemed so barely alive. "Is he—uh—pretty old?"

"Sixteen," the old man said. "Yep, that's pretty old for a dog. 'Specially a hunter like Chief…we've had some high times together, haven't we, old boy?"

The tail thumped once again. Amanda knelt gingerly[22] and stroked the black coat; it was silky soft, but there seemed nothing between it and the bones beneath. To cover her dismay, she said hurriedly, "I guess a dog is a pretty good friend, isn't he?"

"The right kind of dog—yep, no better."

"You mean, like a hunter maybe?"

The old man snorted. "Breed's the least of it! Line up a hundred Labradors[23] and, chances are, you wouldn't find another like Chief. Wasn't another in his own litter like him. I know—I had the pick of the litter."

Grunting a little with the effort, he straightened and moved to a chair by an ancient roll-top desk. "My friend couldn't figure why I took the pup

---

21. *dappling* (DAP ling): a sprinkling of spots
22. *gingerly* (JIN jer lee): delicately, with care and caution
23. *labradors* (LAB ruh dorz): a breed of dog

I did. 'Sam,' he says, 'that's the runt of the lot! Look here—see how lively this one is!' But I held to my choice—yes siree, I knew I had a winner."

"How?" asked Amanda, fascinated.

"By the look in his eyes. There he sat, all paws and floppy head, as forlorn[24] a pup as you'd see by any ash can, but those eyes were watching me. 'Believe in me,' they said, 'and I can do anything.' " The old man laughed. "Guess you think I'm a little foolish—well, maybe so. But I wasn't wrong about Chief, no sir! This proves it."

The old desk creaked as he rolled up the cover. In every pigeonhole[25] within there was a ribbon—red ribbons, blue ribbons, purple ribbons, and a single gold medal. "Won 'em all, Chief did," the old man said proudly. He touched one after another. "Best working dog...best in class...best of show..."

Out of curiosity, Amanda reached for the gold medal. "Why, it's a *runner's* medal!" she cried.

The old man took the medal from her and studied it fondly. "Yep, this was his first—bought it myself. Chief cried his heart out that day, wanted to do miracles for me but he just didn't have the know-how yet. 'Never you mind,' I told him. '*I* know you're a champion.' Next time I went to town, I bought him a medal to wear till he'd proved himself to everyone else."

As if he had followed their conversation, the black dog thumped his tail once more, and fleetingly raised his head. The old man nodded. "Yep, you're right, Chief. You showed 'em. Don't need this one anymore."

Unexpectedly, he extended it to Amanda. "*You* wear it, Sis. You got the look—just like Chief had. Wear it till you win your own."

Amanda gulped. She sniffed back tears and had to rub her nose childishly. "They look at me—" she sobbed, "but they don't *see* me!"

"You see yourself, don't you?" the old man asked mildly. "Well, then, what more do you need? A dream, and the ambition to work for it—enough for anybody." Gently he closed her fingers over the medal.

---

24. *forlorn* (for LORN): feeling lost and sad

25. *pigeonhole* (PIJ un hole): a small compartment in a desk used for storing letters, papers, or other small items

Thinking It Over

1. Amanda exclaims, "Mom, I'm not a *baby!*" What is Amanda really trying to tell her mother?

2. Amanda is attending a new school this fall. She does not yet have any close friends. How does that feel?

3. You have been told to behave well, because you represent a particular group, or because your parents want people to think well of your family. How does it feel? (Write your answer in the first person and the present tense. It should be at least a paragraph of several sentences.)

4. Amanda feels that no one knows her. Look up the word *know* in the dictionary. What does it mean, to be known? In your life, who really knows who you are?

5. What does the old man think is the solution to Amanda's despair?

Consider This...

When a person behaves badly—in a way that angers or disappoints us—we are supposed to give that person the benefit of the doubt. But what if they keep behaving hurtfully?

In *The Long Winter*, we see a father who repeatedly says hurtful words to his son. He treats his son with scorn. How are we to understand the father's behavior?

We are all human. We know that each of us has failings. Yet as we read the story, we want to pass judgment on the father. Over and over again, he is cruel to his son. Then, when his son has not yet come home, Ralph McKeever orders his foreman to abandon the injured and frightened colt that his son has hand-raised. "Turn him out, I said. Let him heal up himself. If he can't, he'll never be my kind of horse."

As you read, you will see that both father and son have recently suffered a grave loss. We recognize that the father is feeling emotional pain. Why does the father hate anyone or anything that needs help? Who *really* is the one frightened in this situation?

This story shows us that there is a connection between emotional pain and striking out at others. Why might losing a loved one make a person want never to love again?

Walter Havighurst

The Long Winter

A thin, cold rain was falling, and the air came down cold from the snow fields on Sheep Mountain. It felt like March, not the middle of May; winter couldn't let go this year. So it looked good to Dan, when he rode into the little park ringed with dripping spruce,[1] to see his father and Gus already dismounted and blue smoke rising in the gray air. Gus threw down an armload of sticks where big Ralph McKeever was feeding a reluctant fire, fanning it with his Stetson.[2]

The boy broke through the fringe of trees, and his father called, "Drag up one of those dead branches, Dan."

He pulled the horse over to a stunted spruce and grasped a dead limb. The wood splintered as he leaned against it, bracing himself in the stirrups. At the rending noise Diablo shied,[3] and the boy was already off balance. He fell hard, with the broken spruce branch under him.

His father, still fanning the fire, didn't look around. "Can't you learn to stay on a horse?" he said.

Dan got up slowly, pushing the dead limb away. Gus dropped his new load of sticks and splashed across the little stream. He headed off the horse, throwing up his right arm—the one with an iron hook on the wrist—while his good hand caught the reins. In a quick hitch he tied them around a sapling.

---

1. *spruce*: a type of pine tree
2. *Stetson* (STET sun): a hat with a broad brim and a high crown often worn by cowboys
3. *shied* (SHYD): threw the rider with a swift, sudden movement

He looked around. "Hurt, Dan?" he asked.

The boy shook his head.

At the fire his father straightened up slowly, putting the Stetson on his head. As he approached, Dan limped away, his thin jaw set. His father went back to the fire. While he fanned the blue smoke into a blaze, the boy came up, dragging the spruce limb.

The rancher snapped off the wood and tossed it on the fire. "Hungry?" he said.

"Yes," Dan answered.

"Hurt yourself?"

"No."

"When I was your age … going on fifteen … "

The boy reached up for another branch. He was almost as tall as the big man in the blue work jacket, now stained dark with drizzle, but he did not have his father's big hands nor his wide shoulders. Dan pulled at the stubborn limb.

"We've got enough wood now," his father said. "You want to camp here all day and night?"

The boy didn't answer. He jammed his stiff hands into his pockets.

Gus came up from the creek with the coffeepot dripping. With his good hand he dumped the coffee in and set the pot in the crackling fire.

"What do you think I saw down there, boss?"

The rancher looked around.

"That young bull's track—fresh," Gus said.

Ralph McKeever scowled at his son. "You must have rode right past them," he said. "Didn't you see anything?"

"They're half in the creek," the foreman said quickly.

"Which way is he headed?"

"Couldn't tell," Gus answered. "Only shows where he crossed over. But I'd say he was heading down."

"We'll separate then," the rancher said, "after we've had some coffee." He went to his horse and unbuckled the saddlebag.

The rain was letting up, and the fire burned briskly around the blackened coffeepot. He laid out the sandwiches and boiled eggs that Indian Mary, muttering to herself, had fixed at daylight.

A brown froth boiled over and hissed onto the fire. Gus pulled the pot off with his hook and poured smoking coffee into the tin cups.

"We'll make a sweep down the mountain," the rancher said. "I'll go over and catch the other fork of the creek. Gus, you take this fork. You drop down the canyon, Son, and follow Sheep Creek. One of us ought to pick him up on the way. We'll meet down at the flats."

Gus rinsed out the coffeepot, scouring it in the sand. He stomped on the fire and doused[4] it with creek water, though the woods were dripping.

"You know where to go, Son?" the rancher said.

"Down the canyon."

"And keep your eyes open. That bull is worth a lot of money."

The rain began to come down harder as the rancher rode off, his slicker[5] gleaming about the wet flank of his horse.

For a little way the foreman and young Dan rode together. Gus had the reins wrapped around his hook; his good hand pointed. "There's his track," he said, "but it don't tell much about where he was going. It fades right out after he got across."

"We might pick it up again," the boy said, "if he followed the creek."

"That's right."

For a minute there was only the crunch of hoofs and the creak of leather. Gus fingered a pinch of tobacco out of his breast pocket and crammed it into his mouth. "Saw you limping," he said. "That foot bother you?"

Dan shook his head. "It caught in the stirrup when I fell," he said. "It just got twisted."

"That canyon trail is rough. Maybe you better take this fork. I'll go down the canyon."

The boy swung around, his thin face tense under the wide brim of his hat. "Dad wouldn't—He told me to take the canyon. I can make it."

"Oh, sure," the foreman said. "But Diablo's spooking today. And your foot—"

"It'll be all right."

"You sure, Danny?"

---

4. *doused* (DOWST): drenched

5. *slicker*: a raincoat

The boy sat rigid in the saddle. Danny—that was what his mother had always called him. He hadn't heard it since that gray day, with the snow swirling furiously against her bedroom window, a week before the holidays.

"I'm all right," he said. He dug his heels in, and Diablo jumped ahead. The spruce boughs[6] rained on him as he made for the head of the canyon.

"See you at the flats," the foreman called.

Ralph McKeever had forded[7] the noisy water and come out on the green flats when Gus appeared, driving the yearling bull ahead of him. Dan was not there. They waited awhile in the rain, looking through the drizzle toward the canyon mouth, letting the horses pull at the wet grass.

"He ought to be here," the rancher said. "It's shorter down the canyon."

"Rougher too," Gus said.

The big man grunted. "That's why I sent him that way," he said. "When I was his age, I knew every gulch[8] between here and Granite Peak. I knew every foot of that canyon—could ride it in the dark. He's got to learn."

Gus put a wad of tobacco into his mouth.

"You know how it was last winter," the rancher said, looking off in the rain. "He took it hard. For a month he wouldn't do a thing but tend that colt in the stable—blankets and hot water, ground oats and warm bran mash!" He turned to the slouching foreman. "But he's growing up now. Did you see him up there by the creek when he fell? It hurt all right, with that dead branch under him. But he wouldn't let me come near." The rancher smiled. "He got up and walked away. Did you see him?"

Gus nodded. "I saw him." He spat a brown stream past his horse's ear.

Daylight was nearly gone; a heavy sky was pressing down on the high, bare slopes.

"Let's be moving," the rancher said. "If he looks around any, he'll see we've been here."

---

6. *boughs* (BOWZ—as in "bow wow"): branches
7. *forded*: crossed a river
8. *gulch*: a deep, narrow valley or ravine

They jogged on along the creek, up a draw, across the big pasture. Through the dusk came a light drumming of hoofs. Then a yearling colt raced beside them, head up, showing the white feather between his pointed ears.

"That colt," the foreman said. "You wouldn't think he'd been sick all winter. I guess Dan wasn't wasting his time. Look at that stride. See how he puts his feet down. He'll make us a horse."

"He looks all right," the rancher said, "if he's got stamina."[9]

They rode through scattered pines to the corral, and when they turned the horses out, the yellow lamplight showed from the house. They washed up at the pump, with a good smell of supper coming from the kitchen door and the radio going. Before they went in, Gus looked across the pasture where the horses were standing in the thin, cold rain.

Old Franz, his wrinkled, red face freshly scrubbed, was already sitting up against the radio that was on full blast. Soon he would take the sheep up to the high parks, where there would be no sound but the wind pouring down the pass and the sheep blatting. He got up and hobbled over to the table. "Where's young Dan?"

"In the box canyon," the rancher said. "He probably lost the trail and had to pick his way."

Indian Mary set food on the table, and they ate with the radio shouting. Ralph made a motion over his shoulder, and Mary turned the knob. Then they ate in silence. When she padded around again, filling the coffee cups, she stopped at the empty place next to the end of the table where Ellen McKeever had sat.

"That boy always hungry," she said, nodding her head so that her big shadow moved slowly on the wall. "He never get full."

"He's empty now," Gus said.

Old Franz nodded. "Hungry as a sheep," he said.

Ralph buttered a square of corn bread before he spoke. "When I was his age, I was out for days in these mountains. He has to learn."

---

9. *stamina* (STA mih nuh): endurance; the ability to keep going despite fatigue, pain, hunger, or the like

Indian Mary stalked back to the kitchen, and there was only the noise Old Franz made, working his toothless gums and swilling coffee. They kept waiting for the sound of footsteps outside, for the door to burst open and a voice half bass and half treble to say, "I'm starved!" But when Old Franz pushed his plate back, there was only the steady dripping outside the window and a rattle in the kitchen, where Mary was poking wood into the stove.

After the cheese and pie and another round of the coffeepot, Old Franz turned on the radio again. "Not so loud," Gus shouted around the stem of his pipe. Ralph leafed through the Durango *Herald-Democrat* and then tossed it down. He filled his pipe, stared at the dark window, and began talking about horses.

"You know why our colts bring the price we get, Gus. They survive on their own."

"That colt, Feather—" the foreman began.

The rancher went right on. "Foaled on the range, born maybe in a snowstorm, chased by coyotes and bobcats before they're a week old—they learn how to take care of themselves. Sure we lose some, but the ones that grow up are real horseflesh. They'll always have stamina."

In the slanting lamplight his face was harsh. One hand held the dead pipe in his mouth, and the other twisted a tobacco pouch till the leather was white. He was talking about horses, but even Indian Mary, moving around the table laying out the breakfast places, knew there were other things in his thoughts. There was his loneliness, his confused concern for the son he had cut himself off from, his memory of Ellen McKeever playing the upright piano at the edge of the lamplight. She had insisted on going to Durango to buy Danny's present, a bridle for the colt he was raising. She was already coughing when they started, and that trip was too much, the long cold ride back made longer when the chains broke in the deepening snow and Ralph worked with numb hands in bitter silence, mending them with a snarl of baling wire. That night, when she began to toss with fever, the telephone was dead. Somewhere in the cold woods the wire was down, though a doctor could never have got there through the drifting snow. All because of a gift.

Ralph held it against his son. And when the boy seemed lost without his mother, Ralph held that against him, too. Now he sat with a dead pipe clamped in his jaw staring at the black window.

"Shut off the radio," Gus said.

When Old Franz didn't stir, Gus jumped up, pushed him out of the way, and turned the knob. Outside, through the dripping rain, came a high-pitched whinny.

"That's Diablo," Ralph said.

Gus was already in the kitchen. He took the lantern from the wall, scratched a match on his metal hand, and turned up the wick. Then he went outside.

Ralph came out after him. At the corral gate they found Dan's horse, with raveled reins and a scarred saddle.

"Fell off again," the rancher said.

"He had a bad foot," Gus said. "It twisted when he fell this noon." He lowered the lantern and looked at the horse's ragged hoofs. "There's a rough stretch halfway up the canyon—that new rockslide."

The rain fell cold on their faces.

"We can't get up there tonight," the rancher said. "We'll have to wait for daylight."

Gus pulled off the scratched saddle and the sodden[10] blanket, and then slipped the bridle off Diablo's head. His good hand made a flat sound on the wet rump, and the horse trotted off in the darkness. Gus heaved the saddle into the dark tack room.

As they walked back to the house, the rancher began, "When I was his age—"

Gus cut in. "He's got matches, and there's shelter in the canyon. He won't try to travel on a bad foot. He's hungry, though; that's sure."

"Do him good," Ralph said sharply. "The kid's got to learn to take care of himself."

Old Franz stuck his head out of the bunkhouse door. "Where's Dan?"

"His horse came in alone," Gus said.

"Where do you think he is?" Old Franz insisted.

---

10. *sodden* (SOD uhn): soaking wet

"He's still in the canyon," the rancher said. "Saddle three horses in the morning. We'll start up as soon as there's daylight."

At breakfast, while darkness was thinning outside the window, Old Franz hobbled in, excited.

"We lost a colt, boss—that new one, out of the roan mare."

"Dead?" Ralph asked.

"Dead as a sheep. Throat slit wide open. And that other colt, Feather—" the old man pushed his battered hat back—"he's cut up bad. Part of the fence is down, above the creek. I found the colt there, scared as a sheep, with the wire cuts on him."

Gus got up. "Where is he?" he asked.

"In the corral," Franz answered. "I brought him in with the others." In the kitchen Mary had a package of sandwiches ready and a Thermos jug of smoking coffee. "That boy be hungry," she said.

"Better fill a jug of water, too," Gus said. The rancher followed him outside.

As they crossed the yard, Gus pointed. The sky was brightening, a band of pale blue spreading over the long saddle of snow on Sheep Mountain. But what Gus pointed to was a thread of smoke showing against the dark spruce slopes above the canyon.

"Halfway up the canyon," Ralph said. "He didn't get far."

Gus nodded. "By that rockslide. Right there is where you'll find him." The rancher looked around. "You not going?" he asked.

"I figured to look at this colt."

The clatter of hoofs began as the men opened the heavy gate. The colt ran stiff-legged, head up, ears rigid, eyes rolling. He stopped on the far side of the corral and stood there sweating in the raw air. When he turned, they saw the torn forequarters and the blackened stripes down his legs.

The rancher went toward him. Snorting, tossing his thin head, the colt ran to the far corner. "Whoa, now! Whoa!" the rancher called, closing in on him. The colt bolted. The man waved his hat, and the colt dodged back, slammed into the fence, and fell. The rancher stepped up, but the colt got his blackened legs on the ground and scrambled up. "Whoa, now! Whoa!" Ralph said again. But the colt flew past him, flinging mud.

Ralph walked back to the gate. "Better turn him out," he said, pushing the hat back on his head.

But Gus stood waiting with a hackamore[11] hooked on his metal hand. "He's hurt bad," he said quietly, his eyes on the trembling colt. "He needs some help."

"It's a waste of time," Ralph said.

Gus walked up slowly, holding his good hand out. "Easy, boy, easy. Easy now." Twice the colt jerked past him, and still Gus followed, his voice going on in that steady, quiet horse talk.

"It's no use, Gus." The rancher went to the tie rack and buckled the saddlebags behind his saddle. When he looked around, Gus had the hackamore on the colt and was studying the trembling forelegs.

"Three deep cuts," he said. "I hope they don't go through those muscles." Still muttering quietly to the colt, he tied the hackamore to the rail.

"Turn him out," Ralph said.

"I'll get some tar on him." Gus hooked the blackened bucket with his metal hand.

"You're wasting time," Ralph said again. There was a new sharpness in his voice. "Turn him out, I said. Let him heal up himself. If he can't, he'll never be my kind of horse."

Gus looked up, the blue eyes thoughtful in his leathery face. "What's galling[12] you, Ralph? Any other time—before last winter—you'd be doing this yourself. What's wrong with you?"

The tall man's face was harsher than ever, and his voice was savage. "Nothing is wrong with me. But you can't make a sound horse out of a soft one. Let him heal himself, if he can."

Gus set the bucket down. For a minute he stood scowling across the corral. Then he pulled back his sleeve and held up his right arm. It showed a worn harness strapped to his elbow and holding a leather collar onto his

---

11. *hackamore* (HACK uh mor): a simple harness used in breaking colts
12. *galling* (GAWL ing): irritating

wrist, with the hook anchored in it. "Your father didn't talk like that when I lost a hand with a stick of his blasting powder," he said. "I was just a boy, and I thought I'd never be any good around horses or cattle with my right hand gone. I was ready to blow. But your father wouldn't let me. He made me think I could be as good as any man." Gus spat at a fence post and turned back to the colt.

"It's a waste of time," the rancher repeated.

"Then I'll do it on my own time. Take it out of my wages." Gus's blue eyes blazed as he hooked up the bucket.

Ralph climbed into his saddle. In a grim silence he rode out the gate, tugging the lead horse behind him.

At the canyon mouth he waded his animals across Sheep Creek and urged them up to high ground on the far side. He stopped there, his eyes searching. The sky was clearing, there was a thin sun now, and all along the west slope the wet spruce glistened. Finally he found the gray-blue thread, thinner now but unmistakable. In the windless air the smoke went straight up, across the pale swath of aspens on the mountain shoulder and the high snows on the ridge. Impatiently he nudged his horse ahead. He was not exactly worried about his son, but something was nagging him.

As he moved on up the canyon, his mind kept going back—not to last winter or any time before that—just back an hour ago, when he had ridden away in anger from the corral gate. Now he saw, as though they were there before him, a calm man and a frightened colt. He saw a maimed hand holding the hackamore and a good hand dabbing a tarred brush at the torn forequarters. He heard a patient voice say: "Easy, boy, easy. Steady, now, steady, steady, steady." In that clear picture, Ralph saw the yearling flinch and stand. He was a proud colt, though he had been frail and awkward. He was a hurt and frightened animal, but he had courage. After this morning he'd be marked, but he'd be strengthened, too.

As Ralph rode on, he heard his own voice following him like an echo. "Let him heal himself…You're only wasting time." And he saw the flash of scorn in the foreman's eyes. He was wrong, dead wrong. And Gus was right.

A realization came to him, and it was like the end of a long and numbing pain: *They don't have to survive alone. They can count on help.* The colts and horses…Gus and young Dan…even grim Ralph McKeever himself.

The sun had burned the ground haze off, and now he looked up at the washed blue sky. He nudged his horse and jogged through a scattering of cedars. In the clear again, he searched for the thread of smoke. All he saw was the rimrock and the huge sweep of the upper slopes.

He cupped a hand to his mouth and called: "Dan!…Dan!"

The fading echo went from wall to wall. Then there was only the small noise of Sheep Creek in the canyon's silence.

He urged his horses up a sharp grade and around a jutting boulder. As it climbed, the trail grew rougher. Then there was no trail at all. There was only a chaos[13] of shattered rock studded by snapped and broken cedars.

"Dan!" he called. "Dan!" Now there was a pleading in his voice.

No answer came except the mocking echo. But his narrowed eyes fixed on an unshattered pine beside a massive boulder. He dismounted, unstrapped the saddle bag, and picked his way over the slide of rock.

He called again, "Dan…"

This time his voice was different, but the huddled figure in the huge rock's shelter did not stir. He stepped across the charred sticks and bent over. "Dan," he said quietly.

At his touch the boy awoke. For an instant his startled eyes showed white. He scrambled to his feet, but at the first step he collapsed. Then Ralph saw the bruised and blackened foot bursting out of a tattered sock.

He slit the sock with his knife and pulled it off. He opened the saddlebag, poured cold water on the sock, and bathed the swollen joint. The boy's eyes opened. He looked at his father as if from a distance.

The older man said, "You've got a bad foot, Dan."

"It—it doesn't hurt."

"Hurt? Why, sure it hurts. It hurts plenty," he said, pouring fresh water on the sock. "It's as big as a feed bag."

The boy looked down and his eyes widened.

---

13. *chaos* (KAY oss): confusion

"But it won't stay that way," Ralph said. "In a few days we'll have you as good as ever."

The boy sank back.

"What I don't see," the older man said, "is how you got this far. Every lurch in the saddle would throw you on this foot."

"I fell off," Dan answered.

"Right here? Where you had firewood and this rock for shelter? That was lucky, Dan."

"No. I crawled here."

The man looked again at his son, and now he saw the scarred hands and the torn clothing. As he dabbed at the ankle, a muscle quivered in his cheek. "We—we saw your smoke first thing this morning."

"Can I have a drink of water?" Dan asked. "I'm thirsty."

"Sure you can. I'm forgetting everything. There's hot coffee here, and sandwiches. Mary knew you would be hungry."

As Ralph unwrapped the package, a grimy hand reached out. The first sandwich went in three huge bites.

"I kept looking for the bull, Dad. Did you find him?"

"Yes, we did. Gus picked him up halfway down the gulch."

"Where is Gus?"

"In the corral. Doctoring your colt Feather. He cut himself on the new fence."

"Bad?" Dan asked.

"Yes, pretty bad. But we can take care of him. He was scared and hurt, but we'll get him over it."

The boy seemed to forget the food in his hands. Slowly his eyes went up to his father. "Dad, if we help him—will he—will he have stamina?"

Again the muscle quivered in the man's gaunt cheek. His deep-set eyes looked squarely at the boy. "Yes, he will, Dan. More than ever." The boy swallowed the last of the sandwich. He rubbed his stomach. "I'm still hungry," he said.

"Well, Mary will know what to do about that. We'd better start home. I'm going to carry you to the horses." His arms cradled the boy. "Easy now. Take it easy. Just put your arm around my shoulder."

Ralph stepped carefully through the broken rock and lifted the boy into the saddle. They started down the trail, taking it slowly, the sun warm as a blanket on their backs.

"You all right?" the man asked. "We can stop and rest—anywhere."

"I'm all right," Dan answered.

They forded the creek and came out on the wide green flats, where the wet grass gleamed in the sun.

A magpie flew over, showing its white chevrons,[14] and from somewhere a bobolink sang his bubbling, ding-dong song over and over.

"Summer is getting here at last," the rancher said. "It's a late season. We had a long winter, but it's over now." He turned in the saddle. "You're not saying much, Danny. What's on your mind?"

The boy smiled. "Oatmeal and corn bread," he said, "bacon and pancakes. I'm starved."

---

14. *chevrons* (SHEV rons): V-shaped stripes

Thinking It Over

1. Why doesn't Dan come home that night?

2. What happens to the colt that Dan has raised? How does Gus respond to the colt's injury and fear? What does Ralph McKeever say?

3. Does understanding why a person is mean help you sympathize with him or her?

4. Are you convinced by the sudden change in Ralph McKeever? What is it that causes the change?

5. How do you feel, when Ralph McKeever says, "When I was his age ... "? Is that sort of statement helpful?

Consider This...

When two people from very different cultures meet, they have a choice. They can focus on how different they are, or they can uncover the many ways in which they are alike.

In *Lost Sister*, a woman named Bessie, who had been kidnapped as a child and raised by Indians, is returned to her white family. Three of her sisters cannot relate to her at all. They live in a narrow, enclosed world that looks down on any culture that is different from their own. It never occurs to them that Bessie might value the culture in which she was raised. The fourth sister, Mary, is different. She looks straight into Bessie's heart and finds the sister she remembers from childhood—a woman who has lived a full, productive life as an Indian wife and devoted mother.

The three sisters are strong and stubborn frontierswomen. Bessie is a strong and stubborn Indian. Had they all looked below the surface, they might have been surprised to find that they had at least something in common. Instead, they remain in their separate worlds of hostility and suspicion, giving up the friendship and mutual understanding that might have been theirs.

Dorothy M. Johnson
Lost Sister

Our household was full of women, who overwhelmed my Uncle Charlie and sometimes confused me with their bustle and chatter. We were the only men on the place. I was nine years old when still another woman came—Aunt Bessie, who had been living with the Indians.

When my mother told me about her, I couldn't believe it. The savages had killed my father, a cavalry[1] lieutenant, two years before. I hated Indians and looked forward to wiping them out when I got older. (But when I was grown, they were no menace any more.)

"What did she live with the hostiles[2] for?" I demanded.

"They captured her when she was a little girl," Ma said. "She was three years younger than you are. Now she's coming home."

High time she came home, I thought. I said so, promising, "If they was ever to get me, I wouldn't stay with 'em long."

Ma put her arms around me. "Don't talk like that. They won't get you. They'll never get you."

I was my mother's only real tie with her husband's family. She was not happy with those masterful women, my Aunts Margaret, Hannah, and Sabina, but she would not go back East where she came from. Uncle Charlie managed the store the aunts owned, but he wasn't really a member of the family—he was just Aunt Margaret's husband. The only man who had belonged was my father, the aunts' younger brother. And I belonged,

---

1. *cavalry* (KA vul ree): a unit of the military that serves on horseback
2. *hostiles* (HAHS tulz): enemies (this word is not commonly used)

and someday the store would be mine. My mother stayed to protect my heritage.

None of the three sisters, my aunts, had ever seen Aunt Bessie. She had been taken by the Indians before they were born. Aunt Mary had known her—Aunt Mary was two years older—but she lived a thousand miles away now and was not well.

There was no picture of the little girl who had become a legend. When the family had first settled here, there was enough struggle to feed and clothe the children without having pictures made of them.

Even after army officers had come to our house several times and there had been many letters about Aunt Bessie's delivery from the savages, it was a long time before she came. Major Harris, who made the final arrangements, warned my aunts that they would have problems, that Aunt Bessie might not be able to settle down easily into family life.

This was only a challenge to Aunt Margaret, who welcomed challenges. "She's our own flesh and blood," Aunt Margaret trumpeted. "Of course she must come to us. My poor, dear sister Bessie, torn from her home forty years ago!"

The major was earnest but not tactful.[3] "She's been with the savages all those years," he insisted. "And she was only a little girl when she was taken. I haven't seen her myself, but it's reasonable to assume that she'll be like an Indian woman."

My stately Aunt Margaret arose to show that the audience was ended. "Major Harris," she intoned,[4] "I cannot permit anyone to criticize my own dear sister. She will live in my home, and if I do not receive official word that she is coming within a month, I shall take steps."

Aunt Bessie came before the month was up.

The aunts in residence made valiant[5] preparations. They bustled and swept and mopped and polished. They moved me from my own room to my mother's—as she had been begging them to do because I was troubled with nightmares. They prepared my old room for Aunt Bessie with many

---

3. *tactful* (TAKT ful): diplomatic; avoiding saying anything that will displease the hearer
4. *intoned* (in TONED): said in a formal, self-important way
5. *valiant* (VAL yunt): courageous; brave

small comforts—fresh doilies everywhere, hairpins, a matching pitcher and bowl, the best towels and two new nightgowns in case hers might be old. (The fact was that she didn't have any.)

"Perhaps we should have some dresses made," Hannah suggested. "We don't know what she'll have with her."

"We don't know what size she'll take, either," Margaret pointed out. "There'll be time enough for her to go to the store after she settles down and rests for a day or two. Then she can shop to her heart's content."

Ladies of the town came to call almost every afternoon while the preparations were going on. Margaret promised them that, as soon as Bessie had recovered sufficiently from her ordeal, they should all meet her at tea.

Margaret warned her anxious sisters. "Now, girls, we mustn't ask her too many questions at first. She must rest for a while. She's been through a terrible experience." Margaret's voice dropped way down with those last two words, as if only she could be expected to understand.

Indeed Bessie had been through a terrible experience, but it wasn't what the sisters thought. The experience from which she was suffering, when she arrived, was that she had been wrenched from her people, the Indians, and turned over to strangers. She had not been freed. She had been made a captive.

Aunt Bessie came with Major Harris and an interpreter, a half blood[6] with greasy black hair hanging down to his shoulders. His costume was half army and half primitive. Aunt Margaret swung the door wide when she saw them coming. She ran out with her sisters following, while my mother and I watched from a window. Margaret's arms were outstretched but when she saw the woman closer, her arms dropped and her glad cry died.

She did not cringe, my Aunt Bessie who had been an Indian for forty years, but she stopped walking and stood staring, helpless among her captors.

The sisters had described her often as a little girl. Not that they had ever seen her, but she was a legend, the captive child. Beautiful blond curls, they

---

6. *half blood*: someone born of one white parent and one Indian parent

said she had, and big blue eyes—she was a fair child, a pale-haired little angel who ran on dancing feet.

The Bessie who came back was an aging woman who plodded in moccasins, whose dark dress did not belong on her bulging body. Her brown hair hung just below her ears. It was growing out; when she was first taken from the Indians, her hair had been cut short to clean out the vermin.[7]

Aunt Margaret recovered herself and, instead of embracing this silent stolid[8] woman, satisfied herself by patting an arm and crying, "Poor dear Bessie, I am your sister Margaret. And here are our sisters Hannah and Sabina. We do hope you're not all tired out from your journey!"

Aunt Margaret was all graciousness, because she had been assured beyond doubt that this was truly a member of the family. She must have believed—Aunt Margaret could believe anything—that all Bessie needed was to have a nice nap and wash her face. Then she would be as talkative as any of them.

The other aunts were quick moving and sharp of tongue. But this one moved as if her sorrows were a burden on her bowed shoulders, and when she spoke briefly in answer to the interpreter, you could not understand a word of it.

Aunt Margaret ignored these peculiarities. She took the party into the front parlor—even the interpreter, when she understood there was no avoiding it. She might have gone on battling with the major about him, but she was in a hurry to talk to her lost sister.

"You won't be able to converse with her unless the interpreter is present," Major Harris said. "Not," he explained hastily, "because of any regulation, but because she has forgotten English."

Aunt Margaret gave the half-blood interpreter a look of frowning doubt and let him enter. She coaxed Bessie, "Come, dear, sit down."

The interpreter mumbled, and my Indian aunt sat cautiously on a needlepoint chair. For most of her life she had been living with people who sat comfortably on the ground.

---

7. *vermin* (VUR min): bugs that infest people's bodies and clothes
8. *stolid* (STAH lid): unemotional; not easily stirred

The visit in the parlor was brief. Bessie had had her instructions before she came. But Major Harris had a few warnings for the family. "Technically, your sister is still a prisoner," he explained, ignoring Margaret's start of horror. "She will be in your custody. She may walk in your fenced yard, but she must not leave it without official permission.

"Mrs. Raleigh, this may be a heavy burden for you all. But she has been told all this and has expressed willingness to conform to these restrictions. I don't think you will have any trouble keeping her here." Major Harris hesitated, remembered that he was a soldier and a brave man, and added, "If I did, I wouldn't have brought her."

There was the making of a sharp little battle, but Aunt Margaret chose to overlook the challenge. She could not overlook the fact that Bessie was not what she had expected.

Bessie certainly knew that this was her lost white family, but she didn't seem to care. She was infinitely sad, infinitely removed. She asked one question: "Ma-ry?" and Aunt Margaret almost wept with joy.

"Sister Mary lives a long way from here," she explained, "and she isn't well, but she will come as soon as she's able. Dear sister Mary!"

The interpreter translated this, and Bessie had no more to say. That was the only understandable word she ever did say in our house, the remembered name of her older sister.

When the aunts, all chattering, took Bessie to her room, one of them asked, "But where are her things?"

Bessie had no things, no baggage. She had nothing at all but the clothes she stood in. While the sisters scurried to bring a comb and other oddments, she stood like a stooped monument, silent and watchful. This was her prison. Very well, she would endure it.

"Maybe tomorrow we can take her to the store and see what she would like," Aunt Hannah suggested.

"There's no hurry," Aunt Margaret declared thoughtfully. She was getting the idea that this sister was going to be a problem. But I don't think Aunt Margaret ever really stopped hoping that one day Bessie would cease to be different, that she would end her stubborn silence and begin to relate the events of her life among the savages, in the parlor over a cup of tea.

My Indian aunt accustomed herself, finally, to sitting on the chair in her room. She seldom came out, which was a relief to her sisters. She preferred to stand, hour after hour, looking out the window—which was open only about a foot, in spite of all Uncle Charlie's efforts to budge it higher. And she always wore moccasins. She never was able to wear shoes from the store, but seemed to treasure the shoes brought to her.

The aunts did not, of course, take her shopping after all. They made her a couple of dresses; and when they told her, with signs and voluble[9] explanations, to change her dress, she did.

After I found that she was usually at the window, looking across the flat land to the blue mountains, I played in the yard so I could stare at her. She never smiled, as an aunt should, but she looked at me sometimes, thoughtfully, as if measuring my worth. By performing athletic feats, such as walking on my hands, I could get her attention. For some reason, I valued it.

She didn't often change expression, but twice I saw her scowl with disapproval. Once was when one of the aunts slapped me in a casual way. I had earned the slap, but the Indians did not punish children with blows. Aunt Bessie was shocked, I think, to see that white people did. The other time was when I talked back to someone with spoiled, small-boy insolence—and that time the scowl was for me.

The sisters and my mother took turns, as was their duty, in visiting her for half an hour each day. Bessie didn't eat at the table with us—not after the first meal.

The first time my mother took her turn, it was under protest. "I'm afraid I'd start crying in front of her," she argued, but Aunt Margaret insisted.

I was lurking in the hall when Ma went in. Bessie said something, then said it again, peremptorily, until my mother guessed what she wanted. She called me and put her arm around me as I stood beside her chair. Aunt Bessie nodded, and that was all there was to it.

Afterward, my mother said, "She likes you. And so do I." She kissed me. "I don't like her," I complained. "She's queer."

9. *voluble* (VAHL yuh bul): with a great stream of words

"She's a sad old lady," my mother explained. "She had a little boy once, you know."

"What happened to him?"

"He grew up and became a warrior. I suppose she was proud of him. Now the army has him in prison somewhere. He's half Indian. He was a dangerous man."

He was indeed a dangerous man, and a proud man, a chief, a bird of prey whose wings the army had clipped after bitter years of trying.

However, my mother and my Indian aunt had that one thing in common: they both had sons. The other aunts were childless.

There was a great to-do about having Aunt Bessie's photograph taken. The aunts who were stubbornly and valiantly trying to make her one of the family wanted a picture of her for the family album. The government wanted one too, for some reason—perhaps because someone realized that a thing of historic importance had been accomplished by recovering the captive child.

Major Harris sent a young lieutenant with the greasy-haired interpreter to discuss the matter in the parlor. (Margaret, with great foresight, put a clean towel on a chair and saw to it the interpreter sat there.) Bessie spoke very little during that meeting, and of course we understood only what the half blood *said* she was saying.

No, she did not want her picture made. No.

But your son had his picture made. Do you want to see it? They teased her with that offer, and she nodded.

If we let you see his picture, then will you have yours made?

She nodded doubtfully. Then she demanded more than had been offered. If you let me keep his picture, then you can make mine.

No, you can only look at it. We have to keep his picture. It belongs to us.

My Indian aunt gambled for high stakes. She shrugged and spoke, and the interpreter said, "She not want to look. She will keep or nothing."

My mother shivered, understanding as the aunts could not understand what Bessie was gambling—all or nothing.

Bessie won. Perhaps they had intended that she should. She was allowed to keep the photograph that had been made of her son. It has been in history books many times—the half-white chief, the valiant leader who was not quite great enough to keep his Indian people free.

His photograph was taken after he was captured, but you would never guess it. His head is high, his eyes stare with boldness but not with scorn, his long hair is arranged with care—dark hair braided on one side and with a tendency to curl where the other side hangs loose—and his hands hold the pipe like a royal scepter.[10]

That photograph of the captive but unconquered warrior had its effect on me. Remembering him, I began to control my temper and my tongue, to cultivate reserve as I grew older, to stare with boldness but not scorn at people who annoyed or offended me. I never met him, but I took silent pride in him—Eagle Head, my Indian cousin.

Bessie kept his picture on her dresser when she was not holding it in her hands. And she went like a docile, silent child to the photograph studio, in a carriage with Aunt Margaret early one morning, when there would be few people on the street to stare.

Bessie's photograph is not proud, but pitiful. She looks out with no expression. There is no emotion there, no challenge, only the face of an aging woman with short hair, only endurance and patience. The aunts put a copy in the family album.

But they were nearing the end of their tether.[11] The Indian aunt was a solid ghost in the house. She did nothing because there was nothing for her to do. Her gnarled hands must have been skilled at squaw's work, at butchering meat and scraping and tanning hides, at making tepees and beading ceremonial clothes. But her skills were useless and unwanted in a civilized home. She did not even sew when my mother gave her cloth and needles and thread. She kept the sewing things beside her son's picture.

She ate (in her room) and slept (on the floor) and stood looking out the window. That was all, and it could not go on. But it had to go on, at least until my sick Aunt Mary was well enough to travel—Aunt Mary who was her older sister, the only one who had known her when they were children.

---

10. *royal scepter* (SEP tur): a rod or wand held by a king
11. *the end of their tether*: an expression meaning they had no patience left

The sisters' duty visits to Aunt Bessie became less and less visits and more and more duty. They settled into a bearable routine. Margaret had taken upon herself the responsibility of trying to make Bessie talk. Make, I said, not teach. She firmly believed that her stubborn and unfortunate sister needed only encouragement from a strong-willed person. So Margaret talked, as to a child, when she bustled in:

"Now there you stand, just looking, dear. What in the world is there to see out there? The birds—are you watching the birds? Why don't you try sewing? Or you could go for a little walk in the yard. Don't you want to go out for a nice little walk?"

Bessie listened and blinked.

Margaret could have understood an Indian woman's not being able to converse in a civilized tongue, but her own sister was not an Indian. Bessie was white, therefore she should talk the language her sisters did—the language she had not heard since early childhood.

Hannah, the put-upon aunt, talked to Bessie too, but she was delighted not to get any answers and not to be interrupted. She bent over her embroidery when it was her turn to sit with Bessie and told her troubles in an unending flow. Bessie stood looking out the window the whole time.

Sabina, who had just as many troubles, most of them emanating from Margaret and Hannah, went in like a martyr,[12] firmly clutching her Bible, and read aloud from it until her time was up. She took a small clock along so that she would not, because of annoyance, be tempted to cheat.

After several weeks Aunt Mary came, white and trembling and exhausted from her illness and the long, hard journey. The sisters tried to get the interpreter in but were not successful. (Aunt Margaret took that failure pretty hard.) They briefed Aunt Mary, after she had rested, so the shock of seeing Bessie would not be too terrible. I saw them meet, those two.

Margaret went to the Indian woman's door and explained volubly who had come, a useless but brave attempt. Then she stood aside, and Aunt Mary was there, her lined white face aglow, her arms outstretched. "Bessie! Sister Bessie!" she cried.

---

12. *martyr* (MAR tur): one who willingly suffers—or even dies—for a cause

And after one brief moment's hesitation, Bessie went into her arms and Mary kissed her sun-dark, weathered cheek. Bessie spoke. "Ma-ry," she said. "Ma-ry." She stood with tears running down her face and her mouth working. So much to tell, so much suffering and fear—and joy and triumph, too—and the sister there at last who might legitimately hear it all and understand.

But the only English word that Bessie remembered was "Mary," and she had not cared to learn any others. She turned to the dresser, took her son's picture in her work-hardened hands, reverently, and held it so her sister could see. Her eyes pleaded.

Mary looked on the calm, noble, savage face of her half-blood nephew and said the right thing: "My, isn't he handsome!" She put her head on one side and then the other. "A fine boy, sister," she approved. "You must"— she stopped, but she finished—"be awfully proud of him, dear!"

Bessie understood the tone if not the words. The tone was admiration. Her son was accepted by the sister who mattered. Bessie looked at the picture and nodded, murmuring. Then she put it back on the dresser.

Aunt Mary did not try to make Bessie talk. She sat with her every day for hours, and Bessie did talk—but not in English. They sat holding hands for mutual comfort while the captive child, grown old and a grandmother, told what had happened in forty years. Aunt Mary said that was what Bessie was talking about. But she didn't understand a word of it and didn't need to.

"There is time enough for her to learn English again," Aunt Mary said. "I think she understands more than she lets on. I asked her if she'd like to come and live with me, and she nodded. We'll have the rest of our lives for her to learn English. But what she has been telling me—she can't wait to tell that. About her life, and her son."

"Are you sure, Mary dear, that you should take the responsibility of having her?" Margaret asked dutifully, no doubt shaking in her shoes for fear Mary would change her mind now that deliverance was in sight. "I do believe she'd be happier with you, though we've done all we could."

Margaret and the other sisters would certainly be happier with Bessie somewhere else. And so, it developed, would the United States government.

Major Harris came with the interpreter to discuss details, and they told Bessie she could go, if she wished, to live with Mary a thousand miles away. Bessie was patient and willing, stolidly agreeable. She talked a great deal more to the interpreter than she had ever done before. He answered at length and then explained to the others that she had wanted to know how she and Mary would travel to this far country. It was hard, he said, for her to understand just how far they were going.

Later we knew that the interpreter and Bessie had talked about much more than that.

Next morning, when Sabina took breakfast to Bessie's room, we heard a cry of dismay. Sabina stood holding the tray, repeating, "She's gone out the window! She's gone out the window!"

And so she had. The window that had always stuck so that it would not raise more than a foot was open wider now. And the photograph of Bessie's son was gone from the dresser. Nothing else was missing except Bessie and the decent dark dress she had worn the day before.

My Uncle Charlie got no breakfast that morning. With Margaret shrieking orders, he leaped on a horse and rode to the telegraph station.

Before Major Harris got there with half a dozen cavalrymen, civilian scouts were out searching for the missing woman. They were expert trackers. Their lives had depended, at various times, on their ability to read the meaning of a turned stone, a broken twig, a bruised leaf. They found that Bessie had gone south. They tracked her for 10 miles. And then they lost the trail, for Bessie was as skilled as they were. Her life had sometimes depended on leaving no stone or twig or leaf marked by her passage. She traveled fast at first. Then, with time to be careful, she evaded[13] the followers she knew would come.

The aunts were stricken with grief—at least Aunt Mary was—and bowed with humiliation about what Bessie had done. The blinds were drawn, and voices were low in the house. We had been pitied because of Bessie's tragic folly in having let the Indians make a savage of her. But now we were traitors because we had let her get away.

---

13. *evaded* (e VAY ded): escaped; avoided

Aunt Mary kept saying pitifully, "Oh, why did she go? I thought she would be contented with me!"

The others said that it was, perhaps, all for the best.

Aunt Margaret proclaimed, "She has gone back to her own." That was what they honestly believed, and so did Major Harris.

My mother told me why she had gone. "You know that picture she had of the Indian chief, her son? He's escaped from the jail he was in. The fort got word of it, and they think Bessie may be going to where he's hiding. That's why they're trying so hard to find her. They think," my mother explained, "that she knew of his escape before they did. They think the interpreter told her when he was here. There was no other way she could have found out."

They scoured the mountains to the south for Eagle Head and Bessie. They never found her, and they did not get him until a year later far to the north. They could not capture him that time. He died fighting.

After I grew up, I operated the family store, disliking storekeeping a little more every day. When I was free to sell it, I did, and went to raising cattle. And one day, riding in a canyon after strayed steers, I found—I think— Aunt Bessie. A cowboy who worked for me was along, or I would never have let anybody know.

We found weathered bones near a little spring. They had a mystery on them, those nameless human bones suddenly come upon. I could feel old death brushing my back.

"Some prospector,"[14] suggested my riding partner.

I thought so too until I found, protected by a log, sodden scraps of fabric that might have been a dark, respectable dress. And wrapped in them was a sodden something that might have once been a picture.

The man with me was young, but he had heard the story of the captive child. He had been telling me about it, in fact. In the passing years it had acquired some details that surprised me. Aunt Bessie had become once more a fair-headed beauty, in this legend that he had heard, but utterly sad and silent. Well, sad and silent she really was.

---

14. *prospector* (PRAHS pek tur): someone searching the ground for gold

I tried to push the sodden scrap of fabric back under the log, but he was too quick for me. "That ain't no shirt, that's a dress!" he announced. "This here was no prospector—it was a woman!" He paused and then announced with awe, "I bet you it was your Indian aunt!"

I scowled and said, "Nonsense. It could be anybody."

He got all worked up about it. "If it was *my* aunt," he declared, "I'd bury her in the family plot."

"No," I said, and shook my head.

We left the bones there in the canyon, where they had been for forty-odd years if they were Aunt Bessie's. And I think they were. But I would not make her a captive again. She's in the family album. She doesn't need to be in the family plot.

If my guess about why she left us is wrong, nobody can prove it. She never intended to join her son in hiding. She went in the opposite direction to lure pursuit away.

What happened to her in the canyon doesn't concern me, or anyone. My Aunt Bessie accomplished what she set out to do. It was not her life that mattered, but his. She bought him another year.

Thinking It Over

1. How does the narrator feel about Indians? Why?

2. What does the major warn the sisters about Aunt Bessie? How does Aunt Margaret respond? How would you describe Aunt Margaret's response?

3. The sisters prepare to meet Aunt Bessie. Write two short paragraphs. In the first, describe what Aunt Margaret was thinking when she met Bessie. In the second, describe what Bessie was thinking when she met Aunt Margaret.

4. The narrator often refers to his mother. How is she different from the aunts?

5. The narrator tells us at the beginning of the story how he feels about Indians. As the story progresses, his feelings towards Aunt Bessie grow and change. Describe the narrator's feelings to Bessie in the middle of the story and, then, his feelings about her at the end of the story.

Consider This...

You may come from a family in which music is one of the important parts of family life. Listening to the music of the great composers is much like reading the classics. These are habits that add pleasure, sensitivity, and another dimension to life.

Father and the "1812" shows us that a common interest is the core of many good friendships. Although members of a family usually have very strong ties to each other, when we share a love for something—from baseball to Beethoven—our bond with one another grows even stronger.

Notice that in spite of the father's many abilities, he has a deep yearning that remains unsatisfied. He loves music. He wants to make music. He manages to bring music and musicians to the center of his life, and so gives his family a taste for the arts.

What should one do, when, like Jahnos Kovach, one is driven strongly in a particular direction?

Todd Rolf Zeiss

Father and the "1812"

My father, Jahnos Kovach,[1] was a bricklayer. He lived in Milwaukee, and in the days before trade unions he was also a carpenter, a plasterer, a plumber, an electrician and a cabinetmaker. He knew how to mend harnesses, set saws, tune pianos, and repair bicycles. He could build a house from foundation to roof, tear apart an automobile and put it together again, and sharpen knives so they would hold an edge.

But most of all he wanted to become a musician.

Grandfather, a locksmith, watchmaker and master gunsmith, disapproved. Music was all right—in its place. There was nothing wrong with listening to the opera over WTMJ on Sunday afternoons or going to the band concerts in Washington Park on holidays. But a man should have a trade—something he did with his hands. And he should have something to show for his efforts when he was done. What had a musician to show when the concert was over?

There were arguments. At first merely disagreements, with a remark here, a comment there, an emphatic gesture or two. The remarks became epithets and the comments grew into tirades. Hands waved in the air. There were shouts, accusations. And one day father left.

But it was already too late. His fingers, bruised and calloused by brick and stone, had no touch for keys, no agility for frets or stops, no feeling for strings. His lips, cracked a thousand times by the winter cold and blistered

---

1. *Jahnos Kovach* (YAH nosh KO vach)

a thousand more by the summer wind, were no good for mouthpieces or reeds. His voice had limited itself to a narrow range between "D" above middle "C" and "A" an octave below, making tenor too high and baritone too low.

His ear was good—excellent, in fact. To him the most complicated scores of Bach, Beethoven and Wagner[2] were child's play. He knew every entrance, release, crescendo and decrescendo[3] by heart.

He could conduct. We watched him many times, my brother and I, in later years when he thought he was alone. Standing before the radio or the Victrola,[4] he would wave his arms in the air, cueing[5] the horns, quieting the strings, bringing in the entire ensemble and, flapping and soaring like an eagle, he would raise the orchestra to a deafening crescendo of cymbals and tympani and chimes. We lay on the floor and peered beneath the curtain which separated the parlor from the hall. We could never keep still for very long and our giggling always gave us away. When he heard us, father would turn round, and we could never be certain what was going to happen next. Sometimes he would scowl ferociously and charge forward, roaring like a bear, his huge calloused hand describing an arc through the air which ended abruptly with a whack on our posteriors as we scrambled in retreat. Other times, however, that same large hand would beckon to us, and father would say, "Come, Jahni.[6] Come, Karl. Come and listen." We would go in. "Hear the horns," he would say, lifting us to his lap. "Listen to the cello play counterpoint.[7] Now it starts to build." A wave of his hand would fill the room with sound, and as his hand rose, the music would rise—up and up it would go, whirling and swirling, higher and higher, carrying us with it. His hand would drop and the music would fall—soft, so soft we could hear his heart beating.

---

2. *Bach, Beethoven and Wagner* (BAKH), 1685-1750; (BAY toe vun), 1770-1827;(VAHG ner), 1813-1883: German composers whose works are musical classics

3. *crescendo and decrescendo* (krih SHEN doe and DAY krih SHEN doe): musical terms meaning increasing in loudness and decreasing in loudness

4. *Victrola* (vik TRO luh): a trade name for a record player or phonograph; any machine that plays records

5. *cueing* (KYOO ing): motioning to them to start

6. *Jahni* (YAH nee)

7. *counterpoint*: a melody composed to be combined with another melody

But there were too many conductors already, and nobody was the least bit interested in one who could not play a single instrument, so father did the next best thing. He bought a three-storied brownstone on Juneau[8] Avenue just a few blocks from the Forstkeller[9] where the symphony orchestra rehearsed, married a woman who was an excellent cook and opened a boarding house with special rates for musicians. Because of the low rates, the musicians came. Because of the wonderful meals, and because mother always had something to eat waiting for them when they returned from a late rehearsal or an evening concert, they stayed.

There were other inducements,[10] too. The price of concert tickets, which the musicians could often get for nothing, was deducted from the rent, and if one of them happened to be out of a job for a week or two, which was often the case, music lessons were considered adequate compensation.[11] As a consequence my brother Karl learned to play the piano, the oboe, and the clarinet, and I the violin, the viola, the cello, and the bass violin.

As his patronage[12] increased, father grew happier and happier. He would come home tired after a hard day's bricklaying or plastering, and the talk with the musicians at the dinner table seemed to revive him. After the meal they would adjourn to the parlor for wine and cigars and the discussion would continue, often until midnight. Sometimes they put a record on the Victrola and discussed orchestration. Other times one of the musicians would get out his violin or sit at our piano (a marvelous old Steinway upright whose tone was the equal of any grand), or a group of them would form an ensemble and play into the small hours of the morning. Karl and I often sneaked downstairs in our pajamas to listen to those impromptu[13] concerts, but mother usually caught us and sent us back to bed where we lay awake for hours, listening to the muted strains

---

8. *Juneau* (JOO no)

9. *Forstkeller* (FORSHT KELL er)

10. *inducements* (in DOOS ments): incentives; rewards offered to persuade someone to do something

11. *compensation* (KAHM pen SAY shun): payment

12. *patronage* (PAY truh nuj): customers

13. *impromptu* (im PROMP too): spur-of-the-moment; done without preparation

as they seeped through the plaster and reverberated[14] along the heavy timbers until, I like to think, the entire house was filled with the spirit of some dead composer.

But in the midst of father's happiness lay a strong sense of frustration. Taking his family to the concert every Sunday was not the same as playing in the orchestra. Hearing his sons play music, although it brought him great satisfaction, was not as satisfying as playing it himself would have been. Being among musicians was not the same as being one of them.

Once he came very close to being one of them. A famous pianist of German extraction[15] whose concert tours always included several performances in Milwaukee and who invariably stayed at our house because he liked the food, planned on one occasion to play several piano variations[16] written by Dr. Prager, the conductor of the Milwaukee Symphony. Because this was to be a surprise (the programs, Dr. Prager was told, were "inexcusably delayed" at the printers, and newspapers carrying announcements of the event listed only "some variations"), and because the variations were still in manuscript and had to be secretly purloined,[17] Herr Schmidt (so I shall call him) had had little time to practice them and required a page-turner. He had intended to use for this purpose his secretary and valet, a slender, dyspeptic[18] Frenchman, but before the concert was to begin, the man became violently ill. He said it was something he had eaten.

Herr Schmidt stalked up and down the parlor in his white tie and tails. "Fifteen minutes before the concert!" he stormed. "If he was going to get sick, why couldn't he at least have given us time to find a replacement? I'll have to cancel the variations; that's all there is to it. My poor friend Prager: what a disappointment! But where can we possibly find a page-turner at this hour?"

---

14. *reverberated* (rih VUR buh RAY ted): echoed
15. *extraction* (ex TRAK shun): descent; ancestry
16. *piano variations* (VAHR ee AY shuns): a series of pieces with the same musical theme but different harmony, rhythm, and melody
17. *purloined* (pur LOIND): stolen
18. *dyspeptic* (dis PEP tik): gloomy and irritable

Father volunteered.

"You are a musician, too?" the pianist asked, somewhat surprised, since father had come home late that evening and was still dressed in his overalls.

"No," father replied. "I am a bricklayer. But I read music quite well and I am certain I can turn pages as efficiently and as quietly as that idiot secretary of yours, who can't recognize good food even when it stares him in the face. Besides," he continued, throwing his great arm around Herr Schmidt's shoulders and turning on his warmest smile which, we used to say, could win a lamb from a wolf, "we were planning a little smorgasbord[19] after the concert in honor of you and Dr. Prager."

Herr Schmidt threw up his hands. Father dashed upstairs and returned a few minutes later, wearing the skinny Frenchman's tuxedo, its sleeves and shoulders bulging, trouser cuffs turned under, and a large safety-pin hidden behind the white tie, fastening the collar.

We hurriedly drove downtown to the Pabst Theatre. The orchestra was already tuning up, and mother, Karl and I just had time to get ourselves seated before Dr. Prager and Herr Schmidt walked onto the stage. They were greeted by warm and sustained applause.

The first half of the concert went well with Dr. Prager, the orchestra and Herr Schmidt performing beautifully the "Concerto in E-flat" by Liszt.[20]

The Prager variations opened the second half of the concert. As father and Herr Schmidt walked onto the stage, Karl and I applauded wildly. All went well, with father proving himself an able assistant. But in the middle of the second variation, the accent pedal began to squeak. The audience stirred. Herr Schmidt, with true professional fortitude, continued as if nothing unusual were happening. But every time he pressed the pedal, it squeaked. Herr Schmidt grew visibly annoyed.

At the end of the variation, father stood up, whispered something to Herr Schmidt and hurried off stage. A moment later he returned, carrying

19. *smorgasbord* (SHMOR gus BORD): a meal at which the guests help themselves to a variety of main and side dishes and desserts that are laid out on a serving table; a buffet

20. *Liszt* (LIST): Franz Liszt, 1811-1886, a Hungarian composer

the toolbox which he always kept in the car. Before anyone could think of pulling the curtain, he was down on his knees beneath the piano, toolbox open, working on the pedal with screwdriver, wrench and oil-can.

Herr Schmidt tested the pedal: it no longer squeaked.

Father closed his toolbox, got up, carried it off stage and returned, brushing dust and sweeping wax from the Frenchman's tuxedo. They continued with the next variation. When it was over, the audience, forgetting for the moment its concert manners, burst into applause.[21] Herr Schmidt rose, bowed, bowed again, and then sat down to begin the next variation. The audience continued to applaud. Herr Schmidt stood, bowed once more, and sat again. The applause continued.

"Kovach!" we shouted. "Kovach!"

Herr Schmidt heard us. He smiled, rose again and extended his hand to father. Father stood up, bowed stiffly, gave Herr Schmidt's hand a rough shake, and sat down quickly. The applause died and they finished the variations.

For father, it was not the same as being a musician. It was true that much of the applause Herr Schmidt had received that evening was meant for father, and that father had saved the concert; but being able to repair a piano, however important it might have been at the moment, was not the same as being able to play it.

In the late 'twenties and early 'thirties Milwaukee became quite well known for its music. Every weekend during the summer there were concerts in the Blatz Open Air Theatre in Washington Park, and as the weather grew colder, the orchestra moved indoors to the Pabst Theatre downtown. Because we had a short concert season and it was easy for our musicians to find work during the off-season at downtown theatres like the Palace and the Majestic, and at jazz spots, we were able to hold within the city itself the solid core of musicians so necessary to a good orchestra. Although we often had guest conductors and guest performers, the orchestra itself had very few itinerant[22] members.

---

21. *forgetting… applause*: it is considered highly improper to applaud before the orchestra has played the entire musical work to be performed
22. *itinerant* (i TIN er ent): traveling from place to place

But music was not consigned[23] only to our musicians. It was everywhere. One could walk down any street in the residential districts and hear a cacophony[24] of instruments practicing scales, exercises and recital numbers. People walking to and from work hummed arias from Puccini's "Madame Butterfly," Mozart's "Magic Flute" or "The Marriage of Figaro." One could hear them whistling the theme from Haydn's "Surprise Symphony." In the winter it was there too, but hushed and muted. Blending with the silent snowfall of a winter night, it lay encased behind closed doors and tightly sealed windows, waiting for spring to set it free again.

For father it was like an eternal winter. His desire to play music, to contribute to the sound of an orchestra, lay dormant[25] like a hibernating animal, restless, stirring with the first pre-dawn of spring.

Musicians came to Milwaukee from all over the world, and soon our orchestra was playing two concerts a week, Saturday evening and Sunday afternoon. Generally one of these concerts, usually the one on Sunday, was directed by a guest conductor.

On one of these occasions the guest conductor was a famous Italian, a very particular and exacting man who had never before been in our city. He had just completed a worldwide tour and the stop at Milwaukee was to be its triumphant close. Instead of the usual two, he was scheduled to direct three weekend concerts, and his concluding selection for the Sunday evening performance was to be Tchaikovsky's "1812 Overture."[26]

The musicians at our house were buzzing with excitement. Some of them were nervous; they had heard of the Italian's incendiary[27] temperament and they feverishly hoped nothing would go wrong. The great maestro arrived on the Thursday morning and immediately plunged the orchestra into a whirlwind of rehearsals. They rehearsed and

---

23. *consigned* (kun SYND): entrusted; placed in their care
24. *cacophony* (kuh KAHF uh NEE): a mixture of clashing sounds
25. *dormant* (DOR munt): asleep
26. *Tchaikovsky's "1812 Overture"* (tchai KOF skee; O ver chur): a musical work by the Russian composer, Peter Ilyich Tchaikovsky, 1840-1893, that is best known for its stirring conclusion that includes real cannon fire and bells
27. *incendiary* (in SEND ee AIR ee): fiery

rehearsed until each number was measure perfect. All went well until Friday evening when they rehearsed the "1812 Overture."

Near the end of the overture, which was written to celebrate the Russian victory over Napoleon and which was to be the grand climax of the maestro's triumphant tour, there is a notation[28] for cannon. "Ordnance[29] is to be fired nineteen times." Our orchestra had no cannon. The young man who headed the percussion section, a tympanist[30] named Otto who lived at our boarding house, planned merely to substitute bass drum and tympani, which was often done. When the first stroke of ordnance fell, Otto pounded the tympani and another fellow beat the bass drum.

The maestro stopped the orchestra. "Where is the cannon?" he asked.

"We have none, sir," Otto replied.

"No cannon?" the maestro asked with cold incredulity. "None, sir," said Otto. "We will substitute bass drum and tympani."

"But the score calls for cannon," insisted the maestro, his voice rising. "Tchaikovsky asks for cannon. And I demand cannon!"

"But, sir—we have none," Otto cried.

"Then get one," the maestro screamed, ending the discussion.

The following morning Otto borrowed father's car and chased all over Milwaukee looking for some sort of cannon. But there was none to be had. At noon he remarked plaintively,[31] "If only I could find something, a shotgun, anything…"

"I have a shotgun," father replied.

It was a marvelous gun. Father had inherited it from grandfather. It was an eight-gauge double-barrel, a journeyman's piece made by grandfather to display his craftsmanship for entry into the gunsmiths' guild. It had external dragon-shaped hammers, a fancy brass triggerguard, engraved Damascus barrels[32] with two tiny ivory beads for sights and an

---

28. *notation* (no TAY shun): written instructions
29. *ordnance* (ORD nuntz): cannon
30. *tympanist* (TIM puh nist): drummer
31. *plaintively* (PLAYN tiv LEE): sadly; mournfully
32. *Damascus* (duh MASS kus) *barrels*: barrels made of Damascus steel—hand-wrought engraved steel with wavy lines in it

ivory butt plate. Its stock and fore-end were of burled walnut, polished smooth as glass. Inlaid on either side of the stock was an ivory dragon and there was a small pewter shield at the wrist, stamped with grandfather's initials, "J.K." Father used it for shooting ducks along the Milwaukee River. But if Otto wished, he would remove the shot from a box of shells and it could be used for the concert.

There was one stipulation; father would have to shoot it himself. It was a family treasure, he explained, and if anything should happen to it…

Otto agreed, and that afternoon he brought father and the shotgun to rehearsal. Out of curiosity, Karl and I tagged along and hid in the wings.

"We could find no cannon," Otto explained to the maestro, "but my friend, Jahnos Kovach, has kindly consented to lend us his shotgun." The maestro smiled. "There is one condition," Otto continued. "The shotgun is a family treasure and Herr Kovach insists that he shoot it himself."

Again the Italian smiled. "Certainly," he replied. "Herr Kovach is a musician, of course?"

"I am a bricklayer," father said with quiet dignity.

"A bricklayer! First there is no cannon; and now, I suppose, I am to have a *bricklayer* playing in my orchestra!"

"I read music quite well," said father, "and I assure you I can play the shotgun."

The maestro was furious. They argued violently. The conductor, jumping up and down and waving his hands in the air, yapped and squeaked like a puppy-dog. Father, standing solidly with his massive arms folded across his barrel of a chest, growled and rumbled in response. As the argument grew more and more heated, Karl and I became more and more concerned. How long could father hold his temper? How long would it be before one of those immense fists descended upon this noisy little creature and…

But a temperamental Italian is no match for a determined Hungarian. In the end, father won. They rehearsed the "1812 Overture."

Bang… bang. Father had fired only two shots of the initial volley of ordnance when the maestro stopped the orchestra.

"Do you call that a cannon?" the Italian asked acidly. "It's not even a pop-gun." The men in the orchestra laughed. Father's leathered cheeks grew red. "It must be louder," the conductor cried, savoring his immediate victory, "much, much louder."

"I can make it louder," father said.

"Then do it," the maestro replied. "And don't fire another shot until you do."

Making the shots louder was no problem. Father merely pulled out the wads in the shells and filled them with a triple load of powder. What bothered him was that he had had no chance to rehearse with the orchestra. The first five shots were to follow with a single measure of one another at a tempo of *allegro vivace*.[33] He would have to load both barrels, fire both, reload, fire both again, reload again and fire one—all within five seconds.

For the rest of the afternoon father retreated to the parlor. We could hear the metronome[34] ticking and father counting, "One and two and a three and four and a one." And each time we could hear the hammers of the shotgun click, the shotgun break and snap shut. But the timing was off. The metronome always came out one beat ahead.

That evening father did not go with us to the maestro's first concert, and when we returned we heard him working on something in the basement. Late that night I remember waking to the faint ticking of the metronome and the snap and click of the shotgun. But I was too drowsy to take serious note of it and rolled over and quickly fell asleep again.

The following morning father said nothing. He accompanied the rest of us to services, which was unusual as he generally let mother take care of the family's religion. But I noted that he was especially devout during the silent prayer.

That afternoon we all went to the maestro's second concert, and although we particularly enjoyed a selection by Dvořák,[35] the concert was

---

33. *allegro vivace* (ah LEG ro vih VAH chay): musical instructions telling the musician to play at a rapid (allegro), lively (vivace) pace
34. *metronome* (MET ruh NOME): a small device that clicks out the beats of a piece of music; musicians use them as they practice to make sure they are playing each note at the right time
35. *Dvořák* (DVOR zhahk): Antonin Dvořák, 1841-1904, a Czech composer

generally a disappointment. When we returned home and the musicians were munching on a light between-concerts-snack mother had prepared, we listened to them grumbling their dissatisfaction with the maestro. He was too severe, they said, too tied to the notations. He gave the music no chance to sing.

That evening father put on the tuxedo he had rented especially for the occasion, slipped his shotgun into its case, and we all headed back to the Pabst Theatre. Our seats were to the right in the front row of the balcony where we could see the entire stage. On the backs of our programs, listed at the bottom of the percussion section we found father's name, Jahnos Kovach, in neat hand lettering. Otto had got hold of the programs, and he and other musicians staying at our house had spent the entire morning printing it on every one.

The musicians filed onto the stage. The oboe sounded his concert "A"[36] and the orchestra began tuning up. The maestro entered and walked to the podium. There was a smattering of applause. I felt a moment of panic, not seeing father on the stage and thinking, perhaps, the maestro had refused him his part. But then I realized there would be nothing for him to do during the first half of the concert and he had chosen to remain backstage. I could imagine him poking into every aspect of theatre apparatus and asking the lighting technicians an interminable[37] stream of questions.

The first half of the concert went well. The audience was appreciative but not over enthusiastic. When the musicians returned after the intermission, father assumed his place with the percussionists at the rear of the stage. He removed his shotgun from its case, carefully examined both barrels to make certain they were not fouled, took out an oil-rag and began polishing the barrels and the stock. He then pulled from his pocket a curious device which looked like a beat strap-hinge with a spring attached and taped it to the breech of the gun.

---

36. *concert "A"*: a note played by one member of the orchestra to which all the musicians tune their instruments
37. *interminable* (in TERM in a bul): seemingly endless

Otto came over and they shook hands. The maestro entered and walked to the podium amid light applause.

As the "1812 Overture" began, father sat quietly, his shotgun across his knees, his arms folded, his sunburned face glowing like a red lantern among the pale faces of the musicians. The overture moved slowly for several minutes and then began to build, gathering momentum for the grand climax. As it did so, father got out his triple-load shells and placed them in a neat row on his music stand, clipping several of them to the device he had taped to the gun. At the entrance of the French horns, father stood up and lifted his shotgun. Mother nibbled on her handkerchief. I looked on anxiously and sat on my hands. But brother Karl, who was still young enough to have supreme faith in his father, sat on the edge of his seat in excited but confident expectation.

With a dramatic gesture, the maestro pointed at father.

Ka-whoom! ka-whoom! ka-whoom! ka-whoom! ka-whoom! The initial volley thundered from the rear of the stage. A great cloud of white smoke engulfed the orchestra and rolled out into the auditorium. For a moment everything stopped.

The conductor waved his arms furiously and one by one the awestruck musicians gathered their wits and began to play again. As the music approached the next cannon shot, the musicians tightened up, the music became pinched and sharp. The maestro tried frantically to wave father off. But father's consummate[38] musicianship, like rare wine bottled for years and at last uncorked, could not be contained.

Ka-whoom! went the shotgun. Everyone jumped. *Ka-whoom! ka-whoom!*

Suddenly the orchestra caught hold. It began to play as it had never played before in a mad attempt to equal and incorporate the shotgun blasts. *Ka-whoom!* The maestro could barely be seen behind the thick curtain of smoke. *Ka-whoom!* The orchestra played without him. *Ka-whoom!* The strings raced wildly up and down. *Ka-whoom!* The horns and trumpets came in. *Ka-whoom!* The tympani and chimes. The

---

38. *consummate* (KAHN sum mit): perfect

orchestra hurled itself through the closing measures of the overture, hammered out the final series of concluding chords, built them up and up to the firm and final statement of the last resolving note.

The audience jumped to its feet with great applause.

When it was all over and we and the musicians had gathered round the table for a late celebration dinner, father stood up, and lifting a glass of his best Hungarian wine in one hand and his concert program in the other, said, "Gentlemen, to music."

Thinking It Over

1. How is it that Jahnos Kovach's sons both become musicians with multiple skills?

2. What does a musician have to show when the concert is over?

3. How do you suppose that someone like Jahnos Kovach—a manual laborer—becomes so highly educated in the arts?

4. If you are able to, listen to a recording of Tchaikovsky's "1812 Overture." In a paragraph of several sentences, describe your reaction to the music.

5. What should determine whether parents allow a son or daughter to pursue a particular career?

Consider This...

It is always a good idea to just *read a story through*, before you start analyzing it. Enjoy it. Experience it. React to it. *Then*, if you want to, or you are required to, you can think about the way it is put together, or what stands out especially about it. The events or the theme or the characters or even the setting may strike you. It may be just the wonderful way the writer writes. Remember: Every good piece of literature has artistic *cohesion*—that is, it all sticks together. A good story is self-contained, like an egg.

What is special in *The House Guest*? The author has managed to breathe life into two characters, through the words of just one of them. When the narrator tells us about the houseguest, the narrator is revealed just as clearly. The two of them—the teenager who tells the story and Bridgie, the young houseguest from Belfast that the narrator describes—come into focus simultaneously.

The second time you read the story, look for the words the narrator uses that sound so much like a teenager, and that give the story its informal tone. But make no mistake: This is a person who is sensitive, caring, and smart. At the end, why does the narrator conclude that Bridgie's District is the world?

Paul Darcy Boles

The House Guest

I'm writing this at the downstairs desk where I do homework or just fool around. It's the same desk Bridgie used to come up to and stand behind sometimes. After a second or so I would feel her standing there. Then I would turn around, making it slow because she's a kid you don't want to scare. She has big dark blue eyes, red hair about the color of the sun before it's really up. She doesn't have much of a chin; her cheekbones are high and like smooth little rocks under the clear skin. She's no beauty. I mean, she's just what she is.

When I turned around and she was there as I'd thought, I would say, "Can I help you, Bridgie?" She would shake her head; she'd just wanted to see if *I* was all right. And when she'd made sure I was, she would just turn around and walk off. My mother and father told me she did the same thing with them: stood and looked at them for a couple of seconds, then walked off... satisfied they were still themselves and handy.

She was only with us for six short weeks. It was one of these red-tape deals through the United States government: you signed up to keep a kid from Northern Ireland in your home as a guest. The idea was to show the kids what America was like, as if anybody could do that even in six years. Anyhow, I was all for it; my brother is an intern and he's working in Rome for a year, and I never had a sister.

The night Bridgie first came, after my parents brought her from the city to our town, she didn't talk much at all. I don't mean she ducked her head or looked awkward or fiddled with her feet or hid behind the furniture. It was just that she clammed up.

She had a small green bag with some extra clothes in it and an old doll that had been whacked around quite a bit. That was the whole works, except for the clothes she wore. Next day my mother took her to a couple of shops in town and bought some new stuff. She still wasn't talking a lot, only pleases and thank-yous, and when my mother took the new clothes out of the boxes to hang them up, Bridgie touched them, very politely, as if they belonged to somebody else and she shouldn't make any fuss. She was nine years old.

At first it kept on being kind of eggshelly around her. You see, we weren't supposed to ask her anything heavy about how things were in the place she'd come from. She'd been born in Belfast, grew up there. She had four brothers and two sisters. She was next to the oldest. Her mother had died a year and a half before and her father took care of the family the best he could.

We got all that from the bunch of statistics that came before we even saw her. The people running this show wanted the kids to "fit easily into the American environment" without being pestered. I guess that was a noble idea, but it left an awful lot you couldn't say or ask.

You can hear a good deal of traffic from our dining room, not anything thunderous, but backfires and people pretending they're A. J. Foyt[1] when they zoom down the street. And a couple of times at dinner when this happened, you could see Bridgie stiffen up. She'd get quiet as a rabbit, and it wasn't even that so much as it was the way she looked out of the corners of her eyes. As if she were searching for a neat, dark place to hide in.

It didn't wreck her appetite, though. I don't mean she was a born pig, I just mean she always ate fast and never left anything on the plate. Oh, sure, my mother is a decent cook, but this was a different thing. I noticed she never asked for second helpings, either, but she'd take them when they were handed to her, even if she looked kind of amazed about getting them.

---

1. *A. J. Foyt*: a race-car driver

It was not until the third day she was with us that she really started to open up a little. We were all sitting around yakking after the evening's parade of news. There had been a picture of a building, or what was left of it, that had been bombed in Dublin. The commentator had said, in that level voice they use for good news, terrible news and in between, that the trouble was moving out of Belfast, that it wasn't "contained" anymore. Bridgie had been sitting straight as six o'clock, hands in her lap, and suddenly she said, "My da was in Dublin the once."

There was a good-sized stop in the talk; then my mother asked, "Did he go on a holiday?"

She gave her head a small shake. She wore her hair in two braids wound tight around her head like pale silk ropes. "Nah, ma'am. He went there in a van to help his mate he worked with down at the docks. His mate was movin' to Dublin. When my da come back he brought us a dog."

"What kind?" I asked. "What'd he look like?"

Her eyes went a pretty fair distance away. "Ah, I was a kid then. I hardly remember ut." She looked around blinking, her eyes that same way, as if she were looking in the fireplace where the fire was jumping around in some pine logs and trying to see backward. Then she said, "But soft he was, with fine ears that stuck up when he was happy." She turned back from the fire and her shoulders went up in little wings, shrugging. "He come up missin' inside the week though. My ma never took to him, him makin' messes and all. But he couldn't o' helped it, so young."

That night after Bridgie had been tucked in bed by my mother in the room next to my parents', I asked my mother whether we could adopt Bridgie or something. My mother said that wasn't possible, she'd already asked about it. Bridgie's family needed her too much, for one thing. There were a lot of those big, iron reasons. After my mother explained them we just sat there thinking about her. I kept wishing it was the kind of world where I happened to be President, or anyhow head of the State Department or something, and could cut through some rules.

The next day was Saturday. My mother took Bridgie into the city for lunch and a show and some sight-seeing. The show was something made for kids, very ha-ha, and my mother said that all through it Bridgie sat without moving and not laughing either, with the buttered-popcorn-and-soft-drink bunch hollering around them.

She liked the Carl Akeley elephants and the stuffed-looking Eskimo families in the Field Museum, but the thing she liked best was a bunch of puppies in a pet-shop window. She had to be just about dragged away. "But we can't get her a dog; it would be too cruel when she had to give it up," my mother said. "She couldn't take it back to Ireland…"

After that my mother took her to one of the mammoth toy stores. She walked her through the doll section, but Bridgie wasn't hot about dolls. "I've got the one already," she said. "Ut's good enough."

Finally they got to the crafts part of the store, and there Bridgie finally found something she was really warm for. It was a big leatherworking set with a lot of colored chunks of leather in red, blue, green and yellow, and the knives and the tooling instruments and all the rest. It was about the most advanced leatherworking set I'd ever seen, and I asked Bridgie if she'd like me to help her get started with it.

"Nah," she said, "I'm quick at the readin' and I can soak in the directions. Don't put yourself out for me."

I wanted to put myself out for her all right, though, so a few nights after that I talked her into going ice skating with me down at the town lake. She didn't exactly skate when we got there, but I pushed her around on the skates I rented for her. After a while it started to snow, and going home I carried Bridgie on my back and she carried my skates. I pranced like a horse in the snow and once I heard her laugh.

But on the porch back home when I was brushing snow off her shoulders she said, "I shouldn't 'a gone. I've missed out a whole night o' my leatherin'."

"That's supposed to be fun too," I said. "Like skating. How're you coming with it?"

"I'm learnin'," she said. "It went slow at the first. Them directions was set down by a blitherin' lump. But now I'm swarmin' around it." Then she said, fast, "Please, I'd like a place to work outside the fine room where I do my sleepin'."

I'd happened to look in that room and see her working, chewing her tongue and frowning and fierce. She'd been so into it she hadn't even seen me. Now she said, "It's not the need o' elbow room, there's plenty o' that. It's I'm afraid o' carvin' up the pretty floor. There's the workshop out in your garage, the one next to where ya keep the ottomobiles. It's even got the heater, if ya could spare the oil for that."

I swept out the workroom and got the heater jets open and working the next morning before I went to school. It was a place I'd spent a whole lot of my own time in as a young child, working like a fiend on my important projects. When I got home that afternoon I found she'd spent most of the day out there; I walked out of the back door and went to the workroom window, but she wasn't inside. Then she came around the corner of the garage from the lane in back of it. Her hair was mussed and she looked as though she'd been doing a hundred-yard dash. "Ah, I had to take me a walk," she said. "Ut gets scrooged up, laborin' so over the bench the many hours."

I started into the workroom to turn off the lights, but she ran ahead of me. "Here, I'll do ut." She flipped them off. I could see she didn't want me to see what she was making. She shut the door. On the way back to the house she said, looking at the ground, "Ya won't peach[2] on me? Ya won't tell? Sometimes I just like swingin' around the neighborhood. I won't get lost and shame ya."

We were almost at the back porch steps. She said, "It's fine, walkin' where ya please. Not havin' to stay in the District."

"District?" I said.

"Ah, that's the boundaries. You don't go past 'em unless you're a fool bent on destruction. The District is where you and your people stay inside of."

I'd never even started to think how it would be living inside a few blocks and not stepping over a line. I did then.

She was out in the workroom the next day after breakfast; my mother told me she came in for lunch and then swept right out again. She did the same thing after dinner till I went out and called her in because it was her

---

2. *peach*: to inform against

bedtime. My mother said she was a little worried about all this hangup with leathercraft, but my father said, "Maybe privacy is the rarest thing we can give her," and my mother gave in to that. I didn't tell them about the walks around the neighborhood; Bridgie could take care of Bridgie, all right.

A couple of days before it was time for her to go back—something we weren't mentioning, any of us—my mother and father sailed off in the evening to visit some town friends. Then about nine-thirty my mother called to tell me they were going to stay longer than they'd planned, and to be sure to get Bridgie in from the workroom by around ten. After that, though, the phone rang again; it was some chatty girl I knew from school and hadn't spoken to lately. It wasn't till we'd finally said good night that I sat up and noticed it was ten-thirty.

I bolted[3] out in the night, down the back porch steps and yelled for Bridgie. There wasn't any answer; the whole night seemed quiet as a piece of white steel. I crunched through the snow that had fallen the day before and looked in at the workroom window. The bench light was off.

A second later, I saw her footprints, leading back to the lane.

Halfway down the lane, though, the footprints started to get mixed up with tire tracks and were harder to make out. But that was all right because by then I could see Bridgie herself. She was easy to spot, down at the end of the lane where the boulevard started and not far from the streetlight, kneeling down beside a ribby old black and tan dog. The dog looked as though it might have had Airedale in it, along with four or five other breeds; on its hind legs it would have been about as tall as Bridgie was.

She didn't turn around, maybe didn't hear me, when I came up closer. She was fitting a new collar around the dog's neck. It was acting pretty patient; she talked to it in a kind of low crooning-scolding way. "Hold your head up," she was saying. "You'll be proud and solid as the Rock of Cashel[4] now, and don't be tryin' to scrape ut off or lose ut. Ut's your ticket to some fine homes. They'll feed ya up. They'll think ya been a pet, they'll b'lieve you're valuable ... "

---

3. *bolted*: ran out suddenly
4. *Rock of Cashel*: also known as Cashel of the Kings; a group of ancient buildings still stand on the Rock; castles used by Irish kings in the 12th and 13th centuries

About that time, she saw me. She gave the green leather collar another pat, just the same, before she stood up. It was tooled with a lot of careful flowers, and I recognized one of the brass buckles from the giant leatherworking set.

"Well, you've caught me out," she said. "That was the last of the leather, so ut's just as well. I fitted out an even dozen creatures. It was hard findin' 'em all, some I had to folla for blocks. But none had the collars before, and now they have. It makes their chances o' havin' a home much grander. You're not angered?"

I didn't say anything. I just stuck a hand down to her and she took it. We went back along the lane. She said, "The collar's a kind o' door key. Ya'd be faster to take in a dog with a collar, wouldn't ya, now?" I still didn't say anything and she looked up at me. "There's no hard feelin's, for the immense cost o' the leatherin' outfit?"

I said, "It's okay, Bridgie."

Then I lifted her up (for nine she doesn't weigh a lot) and carried her home.

Before she went up to bed she said, "You're glad o' me? You'll ask me back some day when ut's allowed by our mutual governments?"

"Sure," I said. I kissed her on the forehead. She grinned quickly and broadly, and said, "Yah! Mush!" then backed away and skipped off and upstairs.

I'm writing this at the desk Bridgie used to come up and stand behind while she looked at me to make sure I was still here. I'm still here. Tonight on the news there were some cut-ins from Belfast: bombings and shootings. A while ago I heard a dog outside in the dark howling a little, then going away. I don't know if it had a collar on or not. I turned around when I heard it, but Bridgie wasn't here, of course. She's back home in her District, but maybe that's not exactly true either... because I think Bridgie's District is the world.

Thinking It Over

1. The narrator of *The House Guest* is a teenager. Write down three characteristics the narrator would attribute to Bridgie.

2. The author tells us that Bridgie, from Northern Ireland, was staying with them for six weeks. "The idea was to show the kids what America was like…" Do you think this can be accomplished in six weeks?

3. Write a brief letter of thanks from Bridgie to the family, after her return to Ireland. Give yourself two or three paragraphs to say what needs to be said. If you are able, try to make your voice sound like her voice. As an aid, you can borrow some of the punctuation and spelling the author uses when Bridgie speaks. Certainly it's a good idea to have Bridgie refer to some of the objects or events of the story.

4. What does Bridgie say about making leather collars for stray dogs?

5. Why does someone who has so little, care so much about other creatures?

Consider This...

The Bet is a powerful and moving story by the world-famous writer, Anton Chekhov. Born in 1860 in Taganrog, Russia, he was the son of an unsuccessful grocer and the grandson of a serf—his family was very poor. Chekhov lived only 44 years; yet, he became a physician, a journalist, a dramatist, a short story writer, and a novelist. His work has been valued for more than a century, and he is considered the "father" of the short story and the modern drama.

Chekhov's short stories, plays, and novels deal with the disappointments, the misunderstandings, and the bad choices that are part of the human experience. Chekhov was able to describe powerful emotions without becoming emotional himself—keeping a distance from the characters and their heartbreaking stories.

His tales are known for beginning with an unexplained situation and ending with another mystifying event. As a character in one of the stories says, "decent Russians like ourselves have a passion for problems that have never been solved."

Most readers will walk away from *The Bet* with many thoughts and suggestions for one or both of the main characters. One of the "problems that have never been solved" is about to be handed to you. What will be your solution?

Anton Chekhov
The Bet

It was a dark autumn night. The old banker was pacing fretfully[1] from corner to corner in his room, recalling to his mind the party he had given in the autumn 15 years before.

There had been many clever people at that party, and there was much good talk. They talked among other things of capital punishment.[2] The guests for the most part disapproved of it. They found it old-fashioned and evil as a form of punishment. They thought it had no place in a country that called itself civilized. Some of them thought that capital punishment should be replaced right away with life in prison.

"I don't agree with you," said the host. "In my opinion, capital punishment is really kinder than life in prison. Execution kills instantly; prison kills by degrees.[3] Now, which is better? To kill you in a few seconds, or to draw the life out of you for years and years?"

"One's as bad as the other," said one of the guests. "Their purpose is the same, to take away life. The government is not G-d. It has no right to take a human life. It should not take away what it cannot give back."

Among the company was a young lawyer, a man about 25. "Both are evil," he stated. "But if offered the choice between them, I would definitely take prison. It's better to live somehow than not to live at all."

"Nonsense!"

---

1. *fretfully* (FRET FULL ee): irritably; nervously
2. *capital punishment*: punishing a person with death
3. *by degrees*: in small stages

"It is so!"

"No!"

"Yes!"

The banker, who was then younger and more nervous, suddenly lost his temper. He banged his fist on the table. Turning to the younger lawyer, he cried out:

"It's a lie! I bet you two million you couldn't stay in a prison cell, even for five years."

"Do you mean that?" asked the lawyer.

The banker nodded eagerly, his face red.

"Then I accept your bet," the lawyer said simply. "But I'll stay not five years but 15."

"Fifteen! Fifteen!" cried the banker. He was now wild, as though he had already won the bet. "Done, then. The people here are our witnesses. I stake[4] two million rubles.[5] You stake 15 years of your freedom."

So this foolish, senseless bet came to pass. At the time, the banker had too many millions to count. He was beside himself with joy. All through dinner he kept talking about the bet. He said to the lawyer jokingly:

"Come to your senses, young man. It's not too late yet. Two million is nothing to me. But you stand to lose three or four of the best years of your life. I say three or four, not 15. You'll never stick the incarceration[6] out longer than that, I can tell you. And they'll just be wasted years. Not the smallest coin do I give you if you leave earlier than 15 years. Why, just think of it! My jail will have no bars, no locks. You'll be able to walk out of it any time you want to, and that thought will be like poison to you. So you will walk out; I know that. Sooner or later, you'll walk out!"

And now the banker, pacing from corner to corner, recalled all this and asked himself:

"Why did I make this bet? What's the good? The lawyer loses 15 years of his life, and I throw away two million. That bet was a mistake. On my

---

4. *stake*: risk

5. *rubles* (ROO blz): the basic unit of money in Russia, similar to the dollar in the United States

6. *incarceration* (in KAR suh RAY shun): imprisonment

part, it was the foolishness of a well-fed man. On the lawyer's part, it was pure greed for gold."

He remembered further what happened after the evening party. It was decided that the "prison" would be in the garden wing of the banker's house. For 15 years the lawyer was not to pass out through its door. He was not to see living people, or even to hear a human voice. He was not to receive letters or newspapers. Musical instruments, however, were to be permitted. He could also read books or write letters, and some other things he could order. He had only to pass his order note through a special window, and a guard would bring anything allowed.

Thus, the smallest details of the bet were discussed and settled. At noon on November 14, 1870, the prison term began. It was to last until noon on November 14, 1885. The lawyer must make no attempt to break the rules agreed upon. Any attempt to escape, even for two minutes, would free the banker from having to pay the two million.

The lawyer's first year, as far as it was possible to judge from his short notes, was one of suffering. He grew lonely and bored. From his wing day and night came the sound of the piano. Short, easy novels were his only reading—light stories, crime, and comedy.

In the second year the piano was heard no more. The lawyer asked only for classics.[7] But by the fifth year, music was heard again. Guards who peeked into his room said that he yawned often and talked angrily to himself. Books he did not read now. Sometimes at night he would sit down to write. He would write for a long time, and then tear it all up in the morning. More than once he was heard to weep.

In the second half of the sixth year, the prisoner began zealously[8] to study languages, philosophy,[9] and history. He fell on these subjects with hunger. The banker hardly had time to get books enough for him. In four years' time, about 600 volumes were brought at his request. And later on, after the tenth year, the lawyer sat before his table and read only the Bible. Then he went on to the history of religions.

---

7. *classics*: great books; books of the highest quality of thought and style
8. *zealously* (ZELL us LEE): eagerly; passionately
9. *philosophy* (fih LAHS uh FEE): the study and analysis of ideas

During the last two years the prisoner read a huge amount, quite haphazardly.[10] He would ask for books on science, and then it would be Shakespeare. Notes used to come from him asking at the same time for books on chemistry, theology,[11] and medicine, as well as for a novel. He read as though he were swimming in a sea among broken pieces of wreckage. In his desire to save his life, he was eagerly grasping at one thing after another.

The banker recalled all this, and thought:

"Tomorrow at noon he receives his freedom. Under the agreement, I shall have to pay him two million. But if I pay, it's all over with me. I shall be ruined forever…"

Fifteen years before he had had too much money to count. But now, he did not know which he had more of, money or debts. He had gambled on the stock market—and lost. He had made business deals that turned sour. The fearless, proud man of business had become an ordinary person, trembling with worry about money.

"That cursed bet!" murmured the old man. "Why didn't the lawyer die? He's only 40 years old. He will take all my money, and then go on and marry and enjoy life. To him, I will look like an envious beggar, and he will say, 'Look, let me help you. After all, I owe my happiness to your money.' Oh, such shame!"

"Ruin and shame," the banker went on. "No—it's too much. Too much for anyone. I must escape ruin and shame, even if he has to die—*even if he has to die!*"

The clock struck three. The banker stood listening. In the house everyone was asleep, and he could hear only the frozen trees whining outside the windows. He put on his overcoat and went out of the house, into the garden, dark and cold. It was raining, and a damp wind argued with the noisy trees. Nearing the garden wing, he called the guard twice. There was no answer. "Good," the banker thought. Evidently the guard had taken shelter from the bad weather. The man was probably sleeping in the kitchen or greenhouse.

---

10. *haphazardly* (hap HAZ urd LEE): in no particular order
11. *theology* (thee AH luh JEE): the study of religion

"If I have the courage to kill this man," thought the old banker, "the guard will get the blame."

In the darkness he groped[12] for the door. It opened without a sound. In the prisoner's room a candle was burning dimly. The prisoner sat by the table. Only his back, the hair on his head, and his hands were visible. Open books lay everywhere—on the table, on the two chairs, on the carpet.

Five minutes passed, and the prisoner never once stirred. "Probably asleep at last," thought the old banker, and he stepped forward. Before him, at the table, sat a man unlike an ordinary human being. It was a skeleton, with tight skin, long curly hair like a woman's, and a shaggy beard. The face was yellow, the cheeks sunken. The hands were so long and skinny that they were painful to look upon. His hair was already silvering with gray, and no one who looked at the thin aging face would have believed that he was only 40 years old. On the table, before his bent head, lay a sheet of paper covered with tiny handwriting.

"Poor devil," thought the banker. "He's asleep, and probably seeing millions in his dreams. I only have to throw this half-dead thing on the bed. Then I'll smother him a moment with the pillow. But first, let's read what he has written here."

His eyes dropped to the paper:

Tomorrow, at noon, I am to have my freedom. I shall have the right to mix with people. But before I leave this room, I want to say a few words to you. My conscience is clear, and I stand before G-d, who sees me. I declare to you that I despise all that most people call the blessings of the world.

For 15 years I have studied earthly life. In your books I hunted deer and sang songs. In your books I climbed Mt. Blanc. I saw from there how the sun rose in the morning... In your books I worked miracles, burned cities to the ground, preached new religions, conquered whole countries...

Your books gave me wisdom. I know that I am cleverer than you all. You are mad, and gone the wrong way. You worship things, not ideas.

---

12. *groped*: felt his way hesitantly

You take falsehood for truth and ugliness for beauty. So do I marvel at you, you who have traded heaven for earth. I do not want to understand you.

To show that I despise all that you live by, I give up the two million I once so desired. Can your money buy wisdom? No. I shall come out of here by my own volition[13] five minutes before noon tomorrow. I shall thus break our agreement.

When he had read this, the banker kissed the head of the strange man. He began to weep, and soon he went out of the wing. Never, not even after his terrible losses in the stock market, had he felt such hatred for himself. Back in his own room, he lay down on the bed, but tears of guilt kept him a long time from sleeping.

The banker slept late the next morning. About noon the poor guard came running to him. The prisoner had escaped! He had walked out into the garden! He had gone to the gate and disappeared!

The banker instantly went with his servants to the wing. Yes, the prisoner was gone. To avoid rumors, he picked up the note on the table. He made two neat folds. And on his return, he locked it in his safe.

---

13. *volition* (vuh LISH un): free will

Thinking It Over

1. What does Chekhov call his two characters? What purpose does it serve for neither protagonist to be named?

2. Which of the characters remains unchanged and which character changes? What quality, in the character who does not change, remains the driving force in all that he does? What quality, in the character who does change, is responsible for the change that takes place in him?

3. It has been said by some literary critics that the two characters represent two extremes of one personality—that the two characters in the story actually symbolize opposing sides of one personality. If this is true, what does it show us about human nature and about life?

4. Solitary confinement is the stated terms of the bet. Would the outcome have been different if the prisoner had been permitted contact with other prisoners, visitors, or the natural world—if he had been permitted to go outside in the garden?

5. At the end of the story, the prisoner is "a skeleton with the skin drawn tight over his bones..." Why? Certainly he was given adequate food and drink! Why do you think he has chosen to look this way?

Consider This...

This story has a timelessness: the setting is never identified, and the enemy goes unnamed. The absence of these details gives the theme power, because the protagonist's feelings—about himself and his place in the world—are not limited to a particular place or time.

How does Corporal Nilson feel about himself? In the very first paragraph, we learn that even *before* this phase of the war began, the corporal's face had been *curiously harassed and marked by strain*. Moreover, we are told that because of the way that he is being escorted to see his commanding officer, he is *driven to the incredible conclusion that at last he ha[s] come to be of value*. Why is it incredible that he has worth? Why, *at last*?

Going to Run All Night has two strong thematic threads: (1) a man is tested who feels he has made no impact on the world around him; and (2) we may succeed—even if we do not believe in ourselves—if we have the courage to persist *in spite of our own doubts*.

Who, or what, is the real enemy here? Why is Corporal Nilson a hero?

Harry Sylvester

Going to Run All Night

They brought him in before the commanding officer, a lieutenant colonel, and stood him there, almost as though he were a prisoner, a slight man, whose face, they now remembered, had been curiously harassed[1] and marked by strain before this campaign[2] had begun. He noticed that they walked on either side as if guarding him, as if, indeed, he were a prisoner or someone valued. And since he could think of nothing he had done or left undone for which they should make him a prisoner, he was driven to the incredible conclusion that at last he had come to be of value.

He looked at the lieutenant colonel, seeing that the officer's face was hardly less harassed than his own. All day, in the midst of the danger which constantly encircled them and intermittently[3] killed some of them, the new legend of the lieutenant colonel's irascibility[4] had grown, so that now, standing before the man, the corporal could wonder he was not ripped up and down with words as scores of men had been that day.

The lieutenant colonel looked at him, blinking and staring, as though making some kind of adjustment from rage to calm. Which it was, perhaps, for to Nilson's amazement he said rather mildly, "They tell me that you used to be a runner, Corporal?"

"Why, yes," Nilson said. "Yes, sir, I mean."

"You used to run distances? I mean road races and such?"

---

1. *harassed* (huh RAST): troubled; disturbed
2. *campaign* (kam PAYN): a series of battles fought for a specific purpose
3. *intermittently* (IN tur MITT int LEE): at intervals; every once and a while
4. *irascibility* (ih RASS uh BILL ih tee): irritability; easily provoked to anger

135

"Yes, sir."

"Ever run in marathon[5] races or anything like that?"

"Yes, sir," the corporal said. He was thinking: There is nothing "like" the marathon. Just the figures alone mean something: 26 miles, 385 yards. "I ran seventh one year in the Boston Marathon." Right after he said it, he could see that the lieutenant colonel was not impressed, that he did not know running seventh in the Boston Marathon was not the same as running seventh in another foot race.

"Well," the officer said, as though making the best of a bad bargain, rubbing his eyes tiredly and slowly with the heels of his hands. "Well, as you know, they've sort of got us over a barrel here. The one radio we still have that is working has been damaged so that we cannot vary the frequency enough to keep the enemy from picking it up rather often."

He went on like that, rubbing his eyes, explaining to the corporal as if the corporal were a general—someone who ought to be told of what the situation was. "We think we can break out at dawn, if we can synchronize[6] our attack with some sort of aid coming from our main forces opposite the point of our own attack. Break through the ring," he said vaguely. Then: "Look! You think you could run across the hills by dark and carry them a message?"

Nilson began to think, for some reason, about how his grandmother used to talk about lightning and how you never knew where or when it was going to strike. Fear was not in him, although for a little while he would think it was fear. His gasp was silent, so that his mouth was open before he began to speak. He said, "Why, I guess so. I mean, I'm not in very good shape. I—"

"But in no worse shape than anyone else here," the lieutenant colonel said. "And you used to be a runner. How long since you stopped active competition?"

"Oh, I was running all the time. Right up until my induction,[7] and even then, when I was still in the States and could get leave, I was competing some."

---

5. *marathon* (MAIR uh THOHN): a long-distance race
6. *synchronize* (SIN kruh NYZ): to cause (two or more events) to happen at the same time
7. *induction* (in DUK shun): becoming an official member of (the army)

The officer nodded. "Well, that's about all. There'll be no written message…in case you might be taken. You'll be picked up by one of our own patrols probably. Just tell them we can't last another day here and that we're going to try to come through at dawn. It's possible they won't believe you. But that's a chance we'll have to take. If they have time, they can send a plane over with a message, to let us know that they understand, although it hasn't been very healthy here for planes. There won't be much trouble getting you through their lines at night. I'll send a guard with you until you're beyond their lines and then you'll be on your own. Just follow the road. The main idea is to get there before dawn. I figure it's thirty-five or forty miles before they'll pick you up. We won't attack for six hours. You think you could make it in, say, five hours?"

"Why, if I was in shape," Nilson said, "I could, maybe, easy."

"Still," the officer said, "you're the best we have. Good luck."

"Yes, sir," Nilson said, and saluted and turned.

Outside, the two sergeants stood on either side of him, and the tall one said, "Well, what are you gonna need?"

"I dunno," Nilson said. "I guess I won't need anything. Maybe I'll take a canteen, maybe not." He knew that thirst for water and the actual need for water were not necessarily the same thing; he was already weighing in his mind the weight of the canteen against the necessity for water.

"Well, let's get going, then," the other sergeant said.

The tall sergeant got Nilson a canteen filled with water, and they moved out into the darkness beyond where the tanks and cars stood in a shallow arc like great animals huddled in the dark.

They were more than halfway across the three-mile plain that separated them from the hills holding the enemy, when Nilson said, "Look, this isn't any good for you two, is it? I mean, if they see us, three isn't going to be much better than one?"

"Stop being noble,"[8] the tall sergeant said. "Someone's got to show you through the hills."

"I see what you mean," Nilson said.

---

8. *noble* (NO buhl): too idealistic and self-sacrificing

It was simpler than he had thought it would be. You could neither hear nor see the enemy, who needed no pickets to hear tanks approaching, or a plane.

The three moved upward over the dry hills, the soil crumbling under foot as they climbed, so that at the crest the sergeants were bushed, panting in the heat and the altitude like animals, and even Nilson was sweating. In the moonlight, below them and to the west and right, they could see the road.

"I guess this is where we get off," the tall sergeant said. "You better get going."

"All right," Nilson said. "I gotta get ready, though."

He undressed in the cloud-broken dark, until he sat there in his shorts and shirt, his socks and shoes and his dog tag. The other sergeant handed him the canteen.

"I'll take a drink now," Nilson said, "and that'll have to hold me. The canteen's too heavy—"

"You take that canteen," the tall sergeant said. "You're gonna need it."

"Look," Nilson said, then stopped. He saw that they did not know about water and running or any violent exercise. You could be thirsty for an awfully long time without actually needing water, but this was no time to start explaining that to them. "Well," he said, "I'll go along then."

"Good luck," they said. They watched him move, still walking down the slope toward the road a half mile away. They thought it was because he couldn't run down a slope that steep, but Nilson was walking until the water was out of his stomach and he could be sure he wouldn't get a stitch when he started to run.

Watching him, the tall sergeant said, "You think he's gonna do any good?"

"No, I don't," the other sergeant said. "Even if he gets through their patrols, he'll drop before he gets to our people—or quit and go hide."

"What do you say that for?" the tall sergeant said.

"Because you're probably thinking the same thing I am!"

In the darkness, the tall sergeant nodded. "We both know we could go along, too, now and hide until this is over, because they're not going to get through tomorrow morning."

"But we go back, instead," the other sergeant said. "And I don't know why."

"I don't know why, either," the tall sergeant said.

Then they turned and began to go back the way they had come.

Nearing the road, the feeling of great adventure began to leave Nilson. Not fear but a sense of futility[9] took him—of his own littleness in the night and the desert that was also the enemy's country. At the edge of the road he paused, although he could not tell why and attributed[10] it to fear. It was not fear so much as an unwillingness to undergo one more futility.

He had not been a very good runner, and he was now thirty-one. Like many of the young men of the Scandinavian colonies in Brooklyn, he had run more because it was a tradition among their people. He had liked it, although after almost fifteen years of little or no glory, he had begun to feel that he was too old to keep losing that often, had begun to realize that, after a while, it did something to a man. Not that it was any fault of his; after all, you'd have to be pretty special to run well Saturdays or Sundays after being on your feet all day as a post-office clerk.

He still hesitated on the edge of the road; there was in his hesitation a quality of sullenness,[11] a shadowy resentment against some large amorphous[12] body or group that somehow had become identified with the long years of defeat.

Without quite knowing what the resentment was, he knew it to be, if not wrong, at least inappropriate now and here. He sighed and at the edge of the road did a curious little exercise that relatives of his also had done three hundred years before in Norway. He bent over, touching his toes five or six times and each time straightening up and flinging his arms wide. The idea was to open his lungs quickly and limber the muscles of his chest and arms. Although he was not a very good runner, he knew all about running; he knew that a man ran as much with his arms as with his legs.

He stepped onto the road and in a reflexive gesture pawed at the crude paving as though it were hard-packed cinders, and the heavy G.I. shoes

9. *futility* (fyoo TILL ih TEE): uselessness; worthlessness
10. *attributed* (uh TRIB yoo tud): said that the cause (of something) was
11. *sullenness* (SULL ihn nuss): gloom and ill humor
12. *amorphous* (AY MOR fuss): shapeless

were the short-spiked ones of the distance runner. He felt sheepish,[13] and in the darkness his mouth twisted into a grin. He began to run.

Almost immediately he felt easier; felt confidence blow through him as though it were his blood; felt that now, at last, he was in his own country, or, more accurately, in his own medium.[14] There are mediums of action that vary with the individual; some feel best moving in an automobile, others on a horse, some walking, a few running or flying.

As he ran, he felt with his feet for the part of the tar-and-gravel road that was best suited to him. The road was slightly crowned in the center and in places pocked lightly by machine-gun bullets from the planes that had gone over it. As on most roads, he found that the shoulder was best for running. It was softer, the spikeless shoes slipped less, and its resilience[15] would save him from shin splints tomorrow. He thought with irony that it was of no importance whether he got the little pains along the shin from bruising or pulling the tendons that held the muscle to the bone. Certainly he would run no more tomorrow, come what might; indeed, there might not be a tomorrow.

This started him thinking of what he called fear—but what was really an ennui,[16] a saturation in himself of having for so many years done things to no purpose. He wondered if this, too, would be to no purpose; if some burial detail, an indefinite number of days from now, would find his twisted body some place along this road.

Then he began to think that it would be worse to get to where he was going and not be believed. There was nothing he could think of to do about that, so he stopped thinking of it. Like many Scandinavians, he was a fatalist,[17] and the war had not helped overcome that.

The night—soft, warm and windless—was all around him. In its blackness, there was a quality of brown; or perhaps he imagined this, for all day the hills were brown, so that afterward you associated the color

---

13. *sheepish* (SHEEP ish): embarrassed and silly
14. *medium* (MEE dee um): a means through which one expresses oneself (such as through art, music or, here, running)
15. *resilience* (rih ZILL yuntz): elasticity; ability to bounce back
16. *ennui* (AHN wee): a feeling that one is tired of life; a dull, bored feeling
17. *fatalist* (FAY tuh list): one who believes that the future cannot be changed, no matter what one does

with thirst, with violence and with the imminence[18] of death. He had discovered, only recently and to his relief, that he was not afraid of death; after all, he had no responsibilities in life, no dependents; disablement,[19] though, was something else.

Then suddenly he began to think of the time he had run seventh in the Boston Marathon; the cold day and the students unexpectedly lining the road at Wellesley, and the tremendous lift they had given his spirit, just standing there, calling to the runners, the wind moving their banners and their bright shirts.

He was running faster, too fast, he thought. He was beginning to breathe hard. It was too early to be breathing so hard; but he knew that would pass soon, and the thing called second wind would come to him. He slackened his pace a little, feeling the weight of the shoes and trying to reject the thought before it took too much form; trying not to think of it.

He began to think of the enemy and where the enemy might be; all around him, surely, but probably not too near the road, because, by night, planes could see a road. Still, there might be patrols knowing a man running steadily by night was a strange and unaccountable thing. But they might never see him; only hear him and the pounding of his feet on the road. So, deviously,[20] his mind came back to the thought which he could no longer avoid: there was only one thing to do, take the G.I. shoes off and run without them.

He slowed gradually until he was walking, and walked perhaps thirty yards before he stopped. Then he sat on the ground and took off his shoes.

When he stood up, he hesitated again. Once, he had lost a shoe and had finished the race, but the cinders had taken their toll of that foot.

The road here was bad, but principally what he feared was stepping on one of the scorpions. He wondered if they were out by night—and then he began to run again.

Now the elements of strangeness about this man running in the night, this Brooklyn Norwegian in a strange land, was intensified by the silence, in which only his regular, heavy breathing made a sound.

18. *imminence* (IM uh nintz): state of being about to happen
19. *disablement* (dis AY buhl ment): permanent injury
20. *deviously* (DEE vee us lee): cleverly and in a roundabout way

Without knowing it, he ran at times in a kind of stupor.[21] The nights of little or fitful sleep, the days of too little food and water, were beginning to affect him, and he began to take refuge from exhaustion and pain in something at times close to unconsciousness.

Twice he passed tanks not far from the road, their crews sleeping, he himself not knowing he passed them. Like a dun[22] ghost, he drifted with the short, effortless stride he had developed over the long years of competition and training. These little spells of semi-consciousness no longer occurred; effort was too much to permit them, too sustained and by now terrible, so that his senses became acute[23] again, his thoughts long-ranging, sharp and filled with color. It was perhaps this return to acute consciousness, induced by pain, that saved him.

He had begun to think of the long dreams of his youth, of passing through lines of people at the end of the Boston Marathon, as he strode in, tired but easily first; of the Olympic Marathon and the laurel wreath he had read of.

Some place there was sound and a hoarse shouting. He could not tell for a moment whether they were in his thoughts or in the reality of the night all around him. Then the sound, now long familiar to him, but still terrible, of an automatic rifle coughing in the night.

He glanced about him, flinching, his eyes, already strained open by the night, trying to open wider, so that the muscles near them hurt. The shouting, the firing were above him—here the road was sunken— behind and to the right.

The firing sounded again, farther away. He neither heard nor felt bullets. In one of those sudden lifts of speed—instinctive and desperate now—with which a distance runner sometimes in the middle of a race tries to break the heart of his opponents, Nilson started to sprint.

The road ran downhill here, and now through the warm, dark night, the little man let his feet shoot out ahead of him, carrying his legs out with the controlled abandon of the cross-country runner going downhill.

---

21. *stupor* (STOO pur): daze; semi-conscious state
22. *dun*: dull grayish brown
23. *acute* (uh KYOOT): sharp

He ran with almost no sound, although he was not aware of this. The shouting and the sound of guns continued behind him. With a faint pleasure, he realized that it was his passing that had alarmed the enemy.

There was an eeriness about him as he moved in the night. Perhaps it was this, perhaps only the adrenalin further secreted in his body by his fear when the shots sounded—but he found a new strength. The legs, the rhythmically moving arms recovered the thing of which, in his boyhood, he and the other runners had made a fetish[24]—the thing called form.

So, going downhill now, the enemy all around him, he experienced a sense of power, as though he were invisible, as though he were fleeter and stronger than anything that could seek to kill or hinder him.

Sweat bathed him, he glistened as though oiled, and there was a slight froth at his lips. He moved with a machinelike rhythm and his eyes—if they could have been seen—might have seemed made.

The road leveled, ran flat for perhaps a quarter-mile, then began to mount again. He became aware of this only gradually. The first change he noted was in himself, first the mind, then the body. The sense of power, of superhuman ability was gone, almost abruptly, his lungs began to hurt badly, and the cords in his neck. He was, he suddenly realized, nothing special; he was Pete Nilson from Brooklyn, and he was bushed; he was just about done.

He shook his head, like a trapped, bewildered animal. The desire, the need to stop was extraordinarily strong in him. He tried an old trick: he tried to analyze his pain, knowing this sometimes made it disappear. There was the pain in his lungs, in his throat, in the muscles of his eyes, but not yet where his arms went into the shoulders, not yet just above the knees where the thigh muscles overlapped.

His stride had shortened with the hill and his body leaned forward. He had not been above quitting in a few races, when he was hopelessly outdistanced, when he had not been trained right, when he had not enough rest the previous week to make him strong.

---

24. *fetish* (FEH tish): an idea to which one is unreasonably devoted

It seemed that he had never been so exhausted as now, and his mind sought excuses to stop. First, came the thought that if only he knew how long he had to run, he might endure it. Twenty-six miles, 385 yards—that was the distance of the Marathon, and in Boston, in Toronto, you always knew within a few hundred yards how far you had come, how far you had to go. But now, no one knew or had known, not within four or five miles. The enemy was in the hills, and the hills were all around the lieutenant colonel and his men, and beyond the hills that held the enemy were more of your own men, some place. So late in his life he learned that it is important to all men in their various endeavors[25] to see an end, to know how far off that end is.

Fatigue blurred his vision and he started to deviate[26] from a straight line, veering slightly from side to side. Although he did not know it, he was beyond the enemy, and had only to combat himself. But he had forgotten about the enemy, and his mind sought reasons to stop, old resentments that could possess the weight of argument. What had they ever done for him? He should have been a sergeant by now.

Anger formed in him: he could not tell its nature or its object. He realized it might be at himself; then, that it was at himself. He must have been crazy, he thought; he supposed that, all his life, his efforts had been directed obscurely toward achieving a sense of usefulness, corrupted sometimes into what was called a sense of glory. And now, close to it, he had almost rejected it.

When the change occurred, the sudden insight, he was on top of a hill and looking down into a plain full of great shadows; there was a paleness in the sky over the shadows. He was on top of this hill, but whether he was running or standing still, he could not tell, for it was as great an effort to stand as to run.

He began to move downhill again, still veering. He sensed, if he did not see, that there were no more hills beyond and that his own people must be somewhere near, perhaps at the bottom of the hill he now descended.

---

25. *endeavors* (en DEV orz): efforts; jobs or goals that are worked at
26. *deviate* (DEE vee AYT): stray from

As he staggered, half-blind in the dim light, to the foot of the hill, he thought of the Athenian runner[27] finishing the first Marathon and, as he collapsed, crying, "Rejoice, we conquer!" Nilson realized how much that image, those words had been with him, influencing him all his life. They heartened him now, sealed the sense of meaning in him.

A sentry challenged as the road leveled out into the plain, and Nilson, not knowing the password, reasoned that this was the place for him to collapse. Pheidippides,[28] finishing the first Marathon, had cried, "Rejoice, we conquer!" but Pete Nilson, thinking this, and finishing his own run, said in a kind of prayer, "Buddy, don't shoot," knelt and quietly fell forward in the dust.

He didn't remember exactly what he said to them, but they took him to another lieutenant colonel. And the miracle was not over. He could not believe it then; all the rest of his life, he could hardly believe it. They believed him. They believed him, and some place near him as he sat stupefied[29] on a canvas stool in a tent, he heard all around him, in the first light, the sound of armor beginning to move, the clatter and roar of the tanks.

A staff sergeant tried to explain. "Look," he said, "nobody comes down here in the shape you're in to lie to somebody else. You see?" Especially the feet, the sergeant thought.

But all Nilson did was sit on the canvas stool and stare.

"Look," the sergeant said again, "you'll get something big for this. Don't you catch?"

Nilson stared at him. He was beginning to catch, but it would be a long time, if ever, before he could make anyone understand. The big thing, the most important thing in his life, was that he had come down here, without credentials[30] of any sort, and they had believed him. The citation, the medal, nothing was ever going to mean that much.

---

27. *Athenian* (uh THEEN ee un) *runner*: a runner who was sent from Athens to Sparta (two cities of ancient Greece) to ask for help in fighting the Persians before the battle of Marathon, some 2,500 years ago

28. *Pheidippides* (fie DIP ih DEEZ): the name of the Athenian runner

29. *stupefied* (STOO pih fyd): shocked; amazed; overwhelmed

30. *credentials* (kruh DEN shulz): formal proof of a person's identity or position

"Look," the sergeant said. "They're getting you a doctor. You want anything now, though? Coffee or something?" Don't the guy know about his feet, he thought.

The little froth still at his lips, Nilson shook his head. He looked like a madman, and the sergeant thought that maybe he was mad. But all Nilson was doing was sitting there listening to the roar and thinking that he, Pete Nilson, had set it in motion. He didn't want anything right then, only to sit there and listen.

Thinking It Over

1. The author writes, "the new legend of the lieutenant colonel's irascibility had grown, so that now, standing before the man, the corporal could wonder he was not ripped up and down with words." What does this mean?

2. Why is the lieutenant colonel interested in speaking with the corporal? Why is he making the best of a bad bargain? Why has the enemy got them over a barrel? What outcome does the lieutenant colonel expect?

3. In fact, why is it that the two sergeants return to camp?

4. Just before he starts his run, Corporal Nilson pauses at the edge of the road. What is he afraid of?

5. When the corporal has reached his destination and is sitting on the canvas stool, what is the big thing? Why?

Consider This...

A story that shows a moral struggle in which good wins out over bad provides each of us with the chance to think about our own behavior. The protagonist in such a story sets an example for us—he or she is victorious over feelings that we are not proud of.

Most of us, at some point in our lives, have been angry at our parents, unfriendly to newcomers at school, rude to strangers, embarrassed by the behavior of a loved one, critical of a person who is different from us, or unwelcoming to a guest in our home. Each of these acts involves a kind of theft: the theft of the respect we owe others and ourselves.

Thus, in our own lives, the feelings and behavior we most need to change are not usually earth-shattering. But whenever we are victorious over unkindness, embarrassment, ignorance, fear, or cowardice, we change the world. Terry Erickson in *Stop the Sun* finds himself struggling. What does he win in the end?

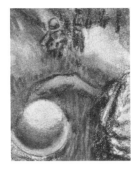

Gary Paulsen

Stop the Sun

Terry Erickson was a tall boy, 13, starting to fill out with muscle but still a little awkward. He was on the edge of being a good athlete, which meant a lot to him. He felt it coming too slowly, though, and that bothered him.

But what bothered him even more was when his father's eyes went away.

Usually it happened when it didn't cause any particular trouble. Sometimes during a meal his father's fork would stop halfway to his mouth, just stop, and there would be a long pause while the eyes went away, far away.

After several minutes his mother would reach over and take the fork and put it gently down on his plate, and they would go back to eating—or try to go back to eating—normally.

They knew what caused it. When it first started, Terry had asked his mother in private what it was, what was causing the strange behavior.

"It's from the war," his mother had said. "The doctors at the veterans' hospital call it the Vietnam syndrome."[1]

"Will it go away?"

"They don't know. Sometimes it goes away. Sometimes it doesn't. They are trying to help him."

"But what happened? What actually caused it?"

---

1. *Vietnam syndrome* is another name for post-traumatic stress disorder. This is an anxiety disorder that can develop after exposure to a terrifying event in which grave physical harm has occurred or was threatened. Traumatic events that may trigger PTSD include violent personal attacks, accidents, or military combat.

"I told you. Vietnam."

"But there had to be something," Terry persisted. "Something made him like that. Not just Vietnam. Billy's father was there, and he doesn't act that way."

"That's enough questions," his mother said sternly. "He doesn't talk about it, and I don't ask. Neither will you. Do you understand?"

"But, Mom."

"That's enough."

And he stopped pushing it. But it bothered him whenever it happened. When something bothered him, he liked to stay with it until he understood it, and he understood no part of this.

Words. His father had trouble, and they gave him words like Vietnam syndrome. He knew almost nothing of the war, and when he tried to find out about it, he kept hitting walls. Once he went to the school library and asked for anything they might have that could help him understand the war and how it affected his father. They gave him a dry history that described French involvement, Communist involvement, American involvement. But it told him nothing of the war. It was all numbers, cold numbers, and nothing of what had _happened_. There just didn't seem to be anything that could help him.

Another time he stayed after class and tried to talk to Mr. Carlson, who taught history. But some part of Terry was embarrassed. He didn't want to say why he wanted to know about Vietnam, so he couldn't be specific.

"What do you want to know about Vietnam, Terry?" Mr. Carlson had asked. "It was a big war."

Terry had looked at him, and something had started up in his mind, but he didn't let it out. He shrugged. "I just want to know what it was like. I know somebody who was in it."

"A friend?"

"Yessir. A good friend."

Mr. Carlson had studied him, looking into his eyes, but didn't ask any other questions. Instead he mentioned a couple of books Terry had not seen. They turned out to be pretty good. They told about how it felt to be in combat. Still, he couldn't make his father be one of the men he read about.

And it may have gone on and on like that, with Terry never really knowing any more about it except that his father's eyes started going away more and more often. It might have just gone the rest of his life that way except for the shopping mall.

It was easily the most embarrassing thing that ever happened to him.

It started as a normal shopping trip. His father had to go to the hardware store, and he asked Terry to go along.

When they got to the mall they split up. His father went to the hardware store, Terry to a record store to look at albums.

Terry browsed so long that he was late meeting his father at the mall's front door. But his father wasn't there, and Terry looked out to the car to make sure it was still in the parking lot. It was, and he supposed his father had just gotten busy, so he waited.

Still his father didn't come, and he was about to go to the hardware store to find him when he noticed the commotion. Or not a commotion so much as a sudden movement of people.

Later, he thought of it and couldn't remember when the feeling first came to him that there was something wrong. The people were moving toward the hardware store and that might have been what made Terry suspicious.

There was a crowd blocking the entry to the store, and he couldn't see what they were looking at. Some of them were laughing small, nervous laughs that made no sense.

Terry squeezed through the crowd until he got near the front. At first he saw nothing unusual. There were still some people in front of him, so he pushed a crack between them. Then he saw it: His father was squirming along the floor on his stomach. He was crying, looking terrified, his breath coming in short, hot pants like some kind of hurt animal.

It burned into Terry's mind, the picture of his father down on the floor. It burned in and in, and he wanted to walk away, but something made his feet move forward. He knelt next to his father and helped the owner of the store get him up on his feet. His father didn't speak at all but continued to make little whimpering sounds, and they led him back into the owner's office and put him in a chair. Then Terry called his mother and she came in a taxi to take them home. Waiting, Terry sat in a chair next to his father, looking at the floor, wanting only for the earth to open and let him drop in a deep hole. He wanted to disappear.

Words. They gave him words like Vietnam syndrome, and his father was crawling through a hardware store on his stomach.

When the embarrassment became so bad that he would cross the street when he saw his father coming, when it ate into him as he went to sleep, Terry realized he had to do something. He had to know this thing, had to understand what was wrong with his father.

When it came, it was simple enough at the start. It had taken some courage, more than Terry thought he could find. His father was sitting in the kitchen at the table and his mother had gone shopping. Terry wanted it that way; he wanted his father alone. His mother seemed to try to protect him, as if his father could break.

Terry got a soda out of the refrigerator and popped it open. As an afterthought, he handed it to his father and got another for himself. Then he sat at the table.

His father smiled. "You look serious."

"Well..."

It went nowhere for a moment, and Terry was just about to drop it altogether. It may be the wrong time, he thought, but there might never be a better one. He tightened his back, took a sip of pop.

"I was wondering if we could talk about something, Dad," Terry said.

"Something pretty heavy, judging by your face."

"Yes."

"Well?"

I still can't do it, Terry thought. Things are bad, but maybe not as bad as they could get. I can still drop this thing.

"Vietnam," Terry blurted out. And he thought, there, it's out. It's out and gone.

"No!" his father said sharply. It was as if he had been struck a blow. A body blow.

"But, Dad."

"No. That's another part of my life. A bad part. A rotten part. It was before I met your mother, long before you. It has nothing to do with this family, nothing. No."

So, Terry thought, so I tried. But it wasn't over yet. It wasn't started yet.

"It just seems to bother you so much," Terry said, "and I thought if I could help or maybe understand it better…" His words ran until he foundered, until he could say no more. He looked at the table, then out the window. It was all wrong to bring it up, he thought. I blew it. I blew it all up. "I'm sorry."

But now his father didn't hear him. Now his father's eyes were gone again, and a shaft of something horrible went through Terry's heart as though he had done this thing to his father, caused his eyes to go away.

"You can't know," his father said after a time. "You can't know this thing."

Terry said nothing. He felt he had said too much.

"This thing that you want to know—there is so much of it that you cannot know it all, and to know only a part is…is too awful. I can't tell you. I can't tell anybody what it was really like."

It was more than he'd ever said about Vietnam, and his voice was breaking. Terry hated himself and felt he would hate himself until he was an old man. In one second he had caused such ruin. And all because he had been embarrassed. What difference did it make? Now he had done this, and he wanted to hide, to leave. But he sat, waiting, knowing that it wasn't done.

His father looked to him, through him, somewhere into and out of Terry. He wasn't in the kitchen anymore. He wasn't in the house. He was back in the green places, back in the hot places, the wet-hot places.

"You think that because I act strange, that we can talk and it will be all right," his father said. "That we can talk and it will just go away. That's what you think, isn't it?"

Terry started to shake his head, but he knew it wasn't expected.

"That's what the shrinks say," his father continued. "The psychiatrists tell me that if I talk about it, the whole thing will go away. But they don't know. They weren't there. You weren't there. Nobody was there but me and some other dead people, and they can't talk because they couldn't stop the morning."

Terry pushed his soda can back and forth, looking down, frightened at what was happening. *The other dead people*, he'd said, as if he were dead as well. *Couldn't stop the morning*.

"I don't understand, Dad."

"No. You don't." His voice hardened, then softened again, and broke at the edges. "But see, see how it was...." He trailed off, and Terry thought he was done. His father looked back down to the table, at the can of soda he hadn't touched, at the tablecloth, at his hands, which were folded, inert[2] on the table.

"We were crossing a rice paddy in the dark," he said, and suddenly his voice flowed like a river breaking loose. "We were crossing the paddy, and it was dark, still dark, so black you couldn't see the end of your nose. There was a light rain, a mist, and I was thinking that during the next break I would whisper and tell Petey Kressler how nice the rain felt, but of course, I didn't know there wouldn't be a Petey Kressler."

He took a deep, ragged breath. At that moment Terry felt his brain swirl, a kind of whirlpool pulling, and he felt the darkness and the light rain because it was in his father's eyes, in his voice.

"So we were crossing the paddy, and it was a straight sweep, and then we caught it. We began taking fire from three sides, automatic weapons, and everybody went down and tried to get low, but we couldn't. We couldn't get low enough. We could never get low enough, and you could hear the rounds hitting people. It was just a short time before they brought in the mortars and we should have moved, should have run, but nobody got up, and after a time nobody *could* get up. The fire just kept coming and coming, and then incoming mortars, and I heard screams as they hit, but there was nothing to do. Nothing to do."

"Dad?" Terry said. He thought, maybe I can stop him. Maybe I can stop him before ... before it gets to be too much. Before he breaks.

"Mortars," his father went on, "I hated mortars. You just heard them *wump* as they fired, and you didn't know where they would hit, and you

---

2. *inert*: not moving or motionless

always felt like they would hit your back. They swept back and forth with the mortars, and the automatic weapons kept coming in, and there was no radio, no way to call for artillery. Just the dark to hide in. So I crawled to the side and found Jackson, only he wasn't there, just part of his body, the top part, and I hid under it and waited, and waited, and waited.

"Finally the firing quit. But see, see how it was in the dark with nobody alive but me? I yelled once, but that brought fire again, so I shut up, and there was nothing, not even the screams."

His father cried, and Terry tried to understand, and he thought he could feel part of it. But it was so much, so much and so strange to him.

"You cannot know this," his father repeated. It was almost a chant. "You cannot know the fear. It was dark, and I was the only one left alive out of 54 men, all dead but me, and I knew that the Vietcong[3] were just waiting for light. When the dawn came, 'Charley'[4] would come out and finish everybody off, the way they always did. And I thought if I could stop the sun, just stop the sun from coming up, I could make it."

Terry felt the fear, and he also felt the tears coming down his cheeks. His hand went out across the table, and he took his father's hand and held it. It was shaking.

"I mean I actually thought that if I could stop the sun from coming up, I could live. I made my brain work on that because it was all I had. Through the rest of the night in the rain in the paddy, I thought I could do it. I could stop the dawn." He took a deep breath. "But you can't, you know. You can't stop it from coming, and when I saw the day light, I knew I was dead. It would just be minutes, and the light would be full, and I just settled under Jackson's body, and hid."

He stopped, and his face came down into his hands. Terry stood and went around the table to stand in back of him, his hands on his shoulders, rubbing gently.

---

3. *Vietcong*: refers to the Communist army the American troops fought in Vietnam
4. *Charley*: the slang name American soldiers gave to the Communist enemy—the Vietcong— during the Vietnam war

"They didn't shoot me. They came, one of them poked Jackson's body and went on, and they left me. But I was dead. I'm still dead, don't you see? I died because I couldn't stop the sun. I died. Inside where I am—I died."

Terry was still in back of him, and he nodded, but he didn't see. Not that. He understood only that he didn't understand, and that he would probably never know what it was really like, would probably never understand what had truly happened. And maybe his father would never be truly normal.

But Terry also knew that it didn't matter. He would try to understand, and the trying would have to be enough. He would try hard from now on, and he would not be embarrassed when his father's eyes went away. He would not be embarrassed no matter what his father did. Terry had knowledge now. Maybe not enough and maybe not all that he would need.

But it was a start.

Thinking It Over

1. What is happening when Terry's father's eyes go away?

2. Why does Terry react with embarrassment, when his father is crawling on the floor at the hardware store?

3. Why doesn't Terry's mother tell him more about what is wrong with his father?

4. Why is it helpful to Terry to have more information about what is happening to his father?

5. What does Terry's father mean when he says "I died because I couldn't stop the sun"?

Acknowledgments

Act of a Hero
"Act of a Hero" from *Violations of the Virgins* by Hugh Garner, © Hugh Garner 1971. Reproduced with permission of McGraw-Hill Ryerson Ltd.

Come of Age
From *One Touch of Nature* by B. J. Chute, published 1965 by E. P. Dutton. Copyright renewed 1993 by Elizabeth M. Roach. Reprinted by permission of Elizabeth Hauser.

The Gold Medal
THE GOLD MEDAL, by Nan Gilbert copyright © 1999 by the Estate; reprinted by permission of the Estate and its agent, Barry N. Malzberg

The House Guest
"The House Guest" from I THOUGHT YOU WERE A UNICORN and Other Stories. Reprinted by the permission of Russell & Volkening as agents for the author. Copyright © 1971 by Paul Darcy Boles, renewed in 1999 by The Estate of Paul Darcy Boles.

Mick Harte Was Here
From MICK HARTE WAS HERE by Barbara Park, copyright © 1995 by Barbara Park. Used by permission of Alfred A. Knopf, an imprint of Random House Children's Books, a division of Random House, Inc.

Of Missing Persons
Reprinted by permission of Don Congdon Associates, Inc. Copyright © 1955 by the Hearst Corporation, renewed 1983 by Jack Finney